ANJA FOERSTER | PETER KREUZ

ANYTHING BUT ORDINARY

ANJA FOERSTER | PETER KREUZ

ANYTHING BUT ORDINARY

A CRASH COURSE IN LATERAL BUSINESS THINKING

Marshall Cavendish
Business

Copyright © 2009 Ullstein Buchverlage GmbH, Berlin

First published in German in 2007 by Econ Verlag as *Alles, außer gewöhnlich: Provokative Ideen für Manager, Märkte, Mitarbeiter*

English translation © 2009 Helen E. Robertson Translations Limited

First published in English in 2009 by

Marshall Cavendish Limited
Fifth Floor
32–38 Saffron Hill
London EC1N 8FH
United Kingdom
T: +44 (0)20 7421 8120
F: +44 (0)20 7421 8121
sales@marshallcavendish.co.uk
www.marshallcavendish.co.uk

Marshall Cavendish is a trademark of

Other Marshall Cavendish offices:
Marshall Cavendish International (Asia) Private Limited, 1 New Industrial Road, Singapore 536196 • Marshall Cavendish Corporation. 99 White Plains Road, Tarrytown NY 10591–9001, USA • Marshall Cavendish International (Thailand) Co Ltd. 253 Asoke, 12th Floor, Sukhumvit 21 Road, Klongtoey Nua, Wattana, Bangkok 10110, Thailand • Marshall Cavendish (Malaysia) Sdn Bhd, Times Subang, Lot 46, Subang Hi-Tech Industrial Park, Batu Tiga, 40000 Shah Alam, Selangor Darul Ehsan, Malaysia

The right of Anja Foerster and Peter Kreuz to be identified as the authors of this work has been asserted by them in accordance with the Copyright, Designs and Patents Act 1988.

A CIP record for this book is available from the British Library

ISBN 978-0-462-09971-2

Printed and bound in Great Britain by
TJ International Ltd, Padstow, Cornwall

YOUR TIME IS LIMITED, SO DON'T WASTE IT LIVING SOMEONE ELSE'S LIFE.

Steve Jobs

CONTENTS

PART 2:
FROM EXECUTIVE OFFICE-HOLDERS TO TRUE LEADERS

THE FIRST WORD: RENEWAL REQUIRED

"And now for the homework. What is the capital city of Iceland? Jessica, please."

Jessica does not have to think for long. The answer comes promptly: "Reykjavik!"

"Very good. Thank you, Jessica. And what is the capital of Australia, Hendrik?"

Hendrik doesn't need much time either. After all, he wasn't born yesterday: "Reykjavik!"

Exactly. If Jessica can get top marks for this answer, it would, after all, be unfair if Hendrik didn't get the same marks with the same answer, wouldn't it? Hendrik already knows what he wants to be one day: a manager. Unfortunately, it's not good, not even adequate, to give the same answer to different questions. Instead, it's a case of "Sit down, zero marks". What applies in school applies even more in management. Stock answers won't get you far. It's no longer enough to be hard-working. Diligence and punctuality are all very well in their way, but they're not enough any more. Honesty and conscientiousness and modesty – fantastic (if true), but no longer sufficient. Especially if what you are doing is the same as everyone else.

Fine, in that case we'll just have to improve. Every day, continuously, all the time. Better, better, better! The sad thing is, however, that you can sit there with glazed eyes and repeat this mantra every day and you still won't have a sure way to success. Because getting a little better every day is standard practice nowadays, it just buys you the admission ticket to global competition, permission to take part in the game. Being better is ordinary, nothing more. The real key, however, is being anything but ordinary. Unique. God dammit, we have to be *different*.

This book will take you on a journey: it will show you that it can be done differently. In every area – government and society, business and management, production and marketing – and by every single one of us. Do something different! And do it differently! Something that's anything but ordinary! Something revolutionary! Because that is the only way to renewal. And renewal, in our opinion, is the truly dominant issue when it comes to heaving ourselves out of the mud in which we have been rolling around for the last twenty years or so.

Of course it's not enough just to be different. You also have to know how or what you would like to be. But it's not that hard. Anyway, you can set that problem aside until you've summoned up the resolution to break with tradition. Because the decisive step nowadays is not just a step forward. At the same time, it also has to be a big step sideways which will take you off the beaten track, into the wilderness, the imponderable, where life becomes exciting again and your original instincts, courage and creativity are in demand. That's where you'll discover what you're made of. And you do want to show that, don't you?

By the way: the capital of Australia is not Sydney, not Melbourne, but Canberra. But either of the first two would at least have been more intelligent answers than – Reykjavik. Seatbelts fastened, we're off!

Anja Foerster & Peter Kreuz

PART **1**

NORMALITY IS THE BANE OF EXISTENCE

CHAPTER 1

THE TRAP: YESTERDAY'S SUCCESS IS TODAY'S ENEMY AND TOMORROW'S KILLER

The scene: the end of a presentation we gave in Munich, not long ago. A man strides boldly up. The suit: grey, three-piece. The neatly parted hair: grey, precise. He is seething with emotion. "Something you said there," he explodes, "I really don't buy it!"

Well done, we think to start with. He is a manager in the strategic planning division of a mail order company – and he very obviously knows his own mind. He tells us that one of the most important tasks in his department is competitive analysis. So when it comes to competition, he knows what he's talking about.

And now we come along, and our presentation claims that a mail order company's competitors include cinemas or mobile phone companies, and stuff like that.

"Sheer nonsense," says our man. His competitors are the handful of other mail order traditionalists, of that he is certain. Anything else is complete rubbish.

"Oh, Amazon. Mere book-shifters ..."

Well, our reasoning seems sound enough: there are competitors lying in wait on the other side of the industry's garden fence, because today's customer is no longer chiefly concerned with covering needs. Come Friday evening, she might ask herself: "Will I browse through my catalogue and order something to wear, or meet a friend and take in a movie, or enjoy a cosy gossip on the phone?" "Completely far-fetched," says Mr Grey.

"What about Amazon?" one of us asks. "Oh, Amazon," the greybeard waves a dismissive hand. "Mere book-shifters ..."

Excuse me? Hello!? The last time this man visited the Amazon website must have been around the year 1998. Or he's one of those managers who are practically strangers to the Web, dictate their emails to their PA, and if they ever hear of an interesting website, ask Miss Jones to print it out for them. We remind him that apart from books, Amazon sells DVDs, cameras, computers, garden furniture, toys, software, sports equipment, DIY tools, trainers, pullovers … No doubt about it, there's a white patch on this man's mental map the size of the Pacific. A few weeks after the Munich presentation, we hear from someone else that his department has been closed down in a restructuring programme. Are we surprised? Not really.

There is no such thing as a successful company

"Nothing succeeds like success" is an old saying. And it's not true. It's not true. It's not true. The truth is, nothing is more dangerous than success. It seduces a self-satisfied manager caste into being content with the status quo. Directors start to believe their own press releases. And they take only a marginal interest in what is happening in the market. Why should they do anything else? After all, they are the industry leaders. And the world outside consists of loyal, trusty troops which will always be theirs to command, thanks to their own superiority. Toyota boss Katsuaki Watanabe hit the nail on the head when he said "arrogance and hubris are the silent killers of businesses".

"We are successful" should be deleted from the manager's vocabulary. There is no such thing as a successful company. There are only companies whose past decisions open up better or worse opportunities for the future. The man who calls himself successful is like someone with an infection during the incubation period. He still feels great, but the viruses are advancing on his organs as we speak. Now would be the best time to start therapy. But of course he waits until he's crawling on all fours. He takes no action at all prior to that point.

Arrogance and hubris are the silent killers of businesses.

Our politicians serve as models in this respect: left wing or right, whoever they may be – they sit through every upturn with hands quietly folded in their laps. It is only when the word "crisis" is on everyone's lips that they pretend to tweak things a bit. Until they arrive at the point where the first glimmer of hope of an upturn makes various interest groups insist that all measures are reversed. The clever thing to do here is to get out in time, write your memoirs and really cash in as a consultant and speaker, elder-statesman style.

According to American leadership expert Warren Bennis, even successful companies can ruin themselves in the future if they continue to behave as they did in the past. Is he right? To answer this question, let's start right at the top, with Grundig, the child of the German economic miracle. When the insolvency administrator gave the electronics manufacturer its quietus in the year 2003, the workforce applauded. Sarcasm? Powerlessness? Maybe simple relief that at last the company had arrived at the point of reality. Company patriarch Max Grundig had tuned that out entirely for years. He went through managing directors like others go through toothbrushes, secured a guaranteed dividend of €25 million per annum for his bling-bedecked spouse, and trampled anyone into the ground who so much as thought aloud about offshore production.

But how could his fitters and welders in the Nuremberg factory compete with 1.3 billion Chinese, who do the same job for a bowl of rice a day? The demand for cheap electronic articles had been satisfied more effectively by others for some years by then. But the self-made man from the south of Germany told himself: nothing can happen to us. We are successful.

Instead of considering how the company could keep up with the rest of the world in future, Grundig simply went on his way as before. Five times his boat rocked and swayed alarmingly. The sixth time, it capsized. Today, Grundig is the own label of a Turkish low-cost producer.

How can anyone compete with Wikipedia?

Sticking with the status quo in good times and hanging around until trends fall off a cliff is by no means a purely German speciality, or even a European one. Why fix it if it ain't broke? That would be the Max Grundig motto. Similarly, the *Encyclopaedia Britannica*, for instance, once the best and most respected encyclopedia in the world, is only a shadow of its former self. With effective direct distribution the publisher was still turning over $650 million in the year 1990, but from there on it went on a steep slide. First, the company missed out on the CD-ROM, then the Internet boom. The guardians of the *Encyclopaedia Britannica*, founded in 1768, dismissed Microsoft's Encarta as kids' stuff. And what could be expected to come of a project like Wikipedia, the free Internet encyclopedia, where any fool could make entries? What's more, the sales team wanted them to go full speed ahead: if you're pocketing $600 in commission for every encyclopedia sold, the last thing you want is a change of course.

In the meantime, the world kept on turning. A recent academic study has shown that Wikipedia contains fewer errors than the *Britannica*, evolved by untold generations of grey-bearded professors. Florian Langenscheidt, himself a publisher of reference books, said of Wikipedia: "How am I supposed to compete with a company that doesn't want to make profits?" All Wikipedia has to do is put out a global call for donations, and millions of dollars flood in so that it can buy new servers or improve the website. If people are happy, even eager, to share their knowledge over the Internet, no market player can possibly earn money with the same product. Self-pityingly laments can be heard from publishers who have failed to understand that reality has long since overtaken them.

Managers are not only allowed to be paranoid – they have to be.

The sad truth is that Britannica could have considered alternatives in good time – before it ended up with its back to the wall. In the age of the Internet, the notion that someone will miss out on his chance of an education if he doesn't own a certain book can no longer be used as a threat. And yet, people love books! They love the book per se, not the knowledge that it contains. Britannica could have gone down that route. It could have done more to diversify its product, develop new series, reposition itself from a working tool to a luxury product steeped in culture. It could have changed from a purchase for life to a collector's edition, offering a look and feel that has become rare in the digital age. But the old business was going so well. And this success was not seen as giving them scope for action, but as a cushion for the company to rest on. Yet the years of record profits would have been the right time for a reorientation, and for the courage to make future-oriented experiments. Once your pockets are empty, it's difficult to impossible to change your strategic direction.

The ex-CEO of AlliedSignal, Lawrence Bossidy, said in an interview with *Harvard Business Review* that the corporate platform would burn whether the flames were apparent or not. And that's exactly what happens. Every company is in constant danger. That is why managers are not only allowed to be paranoid – they have to be. Their stalkers are rarely a product of the imagination, but very real. Paranoia can even be good for your health. That's why Boeing chief James McNerney says: "It's my job to keep everybody paranoid."

Incremental improvement is innovation's worst enemy

But does it have to be revolution every time? We always hear the same old tune after our presentations: isn't it better to be a cautious follower than the first mover? Isn't it enough to make incremental improvements? Doesn't the customer always want the same products, but better?

Yes – but! Of course, you can keep your customers happy for a while with incremental improvements, and save your neck that way for the time being. But the question is: how sustainable will these measures be? And are they still right for our times, when opportunities come and go with the speed of light?

After German retail giant KarstadtQuelle AG declared 2001 "the best year in the group's history", the company didn't exactly rest on its laurels. Its in-house bank even made a big hit by offering a free credit card to anyone. At the same time, the company went on a spending spree and acquired equity holdings from every department – TV sports channel Deutsches Sportfernsehen, Golf House, Starbucks in Germany. The one problem was that nobody rattled the cage of its out-dated business model. In old-fashioned, 1970s-style department stores, the last remnants of a sales staff cut to the bone to reduce costs played hide-and-seek with the customers. In the end, the only ones who would join in the game were pensioners and economic migrants. All the others did their shopping on e-Bay, for example. It took go-getter Thomas Middelhoff, who joined the group as CEO in 2004, to make clear to Karstadt that its department store concept would only have a future if it offered buyers a unique experience.

But why on earth does everyone find it so hard to leave the beaten track? Why do so many individuals stick rigidly to what scientists call the "competence path", in other words, yesterday's recipe for success? Because managers behave the same way as experimental animals. If you give a laboratory mouse five channels, and place a piece of cheese in a different channel every day, the mouse will search for its food every day. But if you then start to put the cheese in Channel 4 every time, after a certain number of days the mouse learns that the cheese is always in the same place. The problem for the little rodent is this: if you then suddenly put the cheese in Channel 2, the mouse runs to Channel 4 and ends up in absolute despair. It never occurs to it to look in the other channels. It has forgotten the search phase, and only internalized the success phase. But it could only find the cheese and save itself from starvation if it was the other way around – if it forgot the successes and remembered the search. Is your company trapped in the

Channel 4 syndrome? Thousands of managers are hunting desperately for the cheese in the place they found it yesterday.

Tomorrow, the cheese will be in a different place. Every time.

It's like this: tomorrow, the cheese will be in a different place. Every time. Because that's just the way the world ticks. Business author Charles Handy illustrates this using the S-shaped sigmoid curve: success goes gradually uphill to the apex of the curve, and then steeply down again. Or to use a different image: nobody can surf for ever on the same wave. The trick is to jump from the crest of one wave to the next in time. And to do it before the wave that is carrying you so beautifully at that moment starts to subside and lose energy.

Charles Handy calls the paradox of success the fact that what made you successful prevents you from remaining successful. And Tom Peters says: "the problem of built-to-last is that it's a romantic notion". We agree entirely with these two leading-edge business thinkers, and would add the following: companies have to forget their successes. Business is a long movie with a lot of highs and lows. No company is chosen by fate to go on being successful tomorrow just because it is being showered with praise by investment bankers and management gurus today. Lufthansa's ex-CEO Juergen Weber once said: "Our biggest threat is not competition, but the fact that success makes us lethargic."

A museum is a museum is a museum? That's what you think!

Thankfully, there are companies and managers who understand that. For example, we recently worked with a manufacturer of dialysis equipment, a successful, technologically top-notch company which is a market leader. Companies like this face a huge temptation to sit back and rest on their laurels. But the managers have not given in to temptation.

Of course they refine the products. But that's only half the story, because the company is not so much at risk from manufacturers whose dialysis equipment is less perfect than its own, but rather from pharmaceutical companies who could develop immunization jabs or tablets that will one day wipe out the need for dialysis equipment, for example. This company's management has realized that the biggest threat to the firm is not the competition they are aware of, but the new player who is currently sitting unremarked on the fringe of the market, looking out for his chance. In the same vein, Olivetti did not get into difficulties years ago because of other typewriter manufacturers, but because a completely new technology came along: the PC. And before that, manufacturers of gas lamps were pushed out of the market by electric light, just as they were at the pinnacle of their success.

The management of this dialysis equipment manufacturer wants to be armed and ready for Day X. Small teams constantly monitor the entire health care market. Other groups are already considering alternative products. What they are thinking about would be taboo in other companies: how could we completely reinvent ourselves? What radically different product could we put on the market tomorrow? To do this, it is enormously important to keep not only minds flexible, but structures and processes as well. Nimble people, an intense exchange of knowledge, lean processes, and non-hierarchical mindsets are utterly essential.

What radically different product could we put on the market tomorrow?

We don't know the precise origin of the following quotation, but we'll use it all the same: "You can improve any business, you just have to keep reinventing it – every day". Glenn Lowry is living proof of its truth. He is the director of the New York Museum of Modern Art, also known to genuine and wannabe art connoisseurs as MoMA. When we were in Berlin in the summer of 2005, we saw a gigantic queue in front of the Neue Nationalgalerie on Potsdamer Platz. This mega-cultural event was part of a brilliant strategy by Glenn Lowry, who is currently busy reinventing the art gallery. The spectacular show in Berlin stirred up plenty of local publicity, and made MoMA the top address in the world for modern art, even in Old Europe. We were quite astonished when we saw what was happening by that time in New York. For the sum of almost $500 million, Yoshio Taniguchi, a Japanese architect with almost no previous international reputation, was remodelling MoMA into a museum of a new kind. Art is being staged here as an entirely new experience. Lowry wants to inspire people who have never been in a museum in their lives. The snide comments of conservative culture critics about the biggest museum shop in the world were to be expected – and left Lowry completely cold.

The real point of this story is that old-style business thinking would have given Lowry no reason at all to plunge himself into such an adventure. When he took over the boss's chair in 1995, MoMA was already the most successful museum in the world, and had been for some time. In a country where the public subsidies poured into culture are actually the merest trickle, what induced him to embark upon a remodelling project costing almost $1 billion, including extensions to the collection? Lowry's take on it in the mid-1990s was that the management had to make sure that the institution remained great. "We need a vision," he said. Whereupon the Supervisory Board members granted $860 million that they didn't have. Not at the time, anyway. But it would have been a bigger risk to do nothing.

It can be done!

So they do exist, the companies that can simply cast yesterday's successes out of their memories. That always search every channel for the cheese. What's more, they exist everywhere. Even Bill Gates says that "Microsoft is always just two years away from failure." Microsoft! Two years! And this guy is sitting on a comfortable market share of more than 90 per cent. What on earth can the rest of us say if even Bill Gates is worried? Or let's take Michael Dieckmann, who took over German insurance giant Allianz and broke it up very thoroughly. Or consumer products manufacturer Henkel, who want to generate at least 30 per cent of all revenues with products that have been on the market for less than three years. It can be done!

The key is strategy. Today, the difference between leaders and laggards is no longer measured in decades, but in a few years and sometimes in months. A survey developed by strategy expert Gary Hamel together with the Gallup market research institute addressed 500 top managers. One of the questions went something like: Which players were best able to exploit changes in their respective branches in the last ten years: new entrants, existing competitors or your own company? The vast majority of respondents said: new entrants. Next question: did the new entrants invent new game rules, or did they score through better implementation? As many as 62 per cent of the top bosses replied: they redefined the game rules.

Examples supporting this statement are legion. Apple, for example, awakened the music industry from a deep sleep with iTunes. Apple, of all companies: a computer manufacturer! But still we hear bosses say things like: "Strategy is the easy bit. Our real problem is implementation."

Well, wake up and smell the coffee! Of course strategy is easy if you stick to yesterday's mindsets. But you can hang as many stockings from your mantelpiece as you like on the evening of 25 December, they won't be filled – though it would have worked beautifully the day before. Even a five-year-old could explain to these managers why you need new strategies when the rules change. The problem is just that so few five-year-olds attend these companies' strategy meetings.

In actual fact, strategy is anything but simple if its goal is business transformation. Management is not about the how, it's about the what. It's about objectives. And then about more objectives. And on top of that, it's about objectives. And then there is a big gap, and then it's about implementation. By that time, it's time to set new objectives.

The council of old men normally gives the oldest counsel.

Over the last few years, we have scanned hundreds of unusually successful companies. We always encountered similar phenomena. In the best companies, for example, the strategy debate is not just the domain of a few elder statesmen. It is entrusted to a heterogeneous group that cares deeply about the future of the company. The reason is obvious: the council of old men normally gives the oldest counsel.

Young people are allowed to have their say, that's another point. They are interested in the future by nature. Clever bosses allow juniors to open their mouths and are not afraid to challenge their own thinking. Next, innovative companies fight self-satisfaction like the plague. There is a sign on the wall at Coca-Cola's headquarters that says: "The world belongs to the discontented." This discontent with itself has kept the soda factory from Atlanta well up in the race for more than 100 years now.

Companies that have mastered this trick never stop searching. The late Anita Roddick, one of the most extraordinary and successful female entrepreneurs of our time, once said: "What I like so much about Body Shop is that we still don't know the rules." In a radically changing world, there are no final answers. That's why thinking from a clean sheet is worthwhile. Ask yourself: if we weren't doing what we are doing here and now, and if we were what we are, what would we do then and where and how would we start again from scratch?

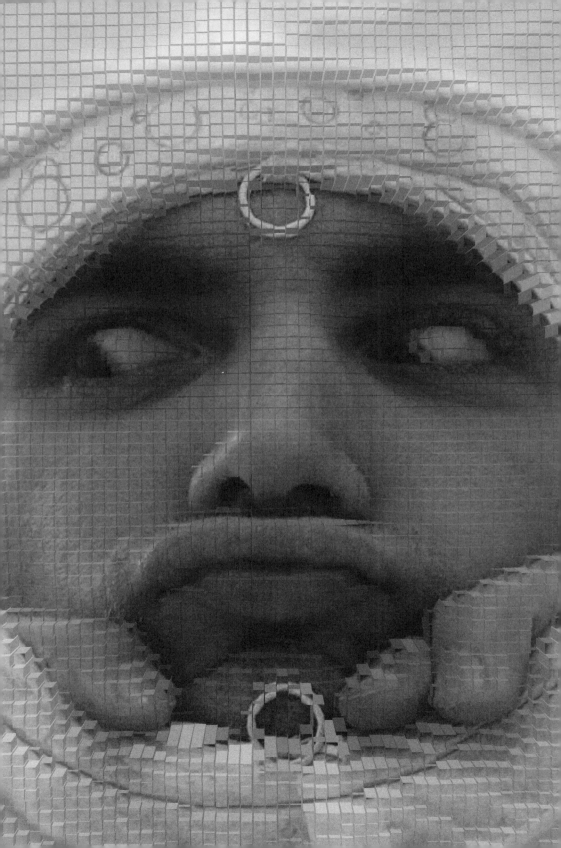

CHAPTER 2

INNOVATION IS MORE THAN NEW PRODUCTS

It's always the same. Whenever and wherever we talk to companies about innovation, we see a sparkle in every eye. They think being innovative is wow, amazing: "Oh, yes, innovations are so important!" – "We have to reinvent ourselves every day!" – "The only thing that endures is change!"

Well, sure, these soundbites trip easily from everyone's tongue. Who wants to be out of the game? Every manager loves to demonstrate how "innovative" and "flexible" he is, and that he "has his finger on the pulse". However, when we look closer and try to find out what innovation actually means in these companies, a different picture emerges ...

When engineers make products

For example, recently we gave a presentation on re-imagining to executives at an industrial company. Reimagining? Fantastic subject! During the presentation, everyone listens patiently. Some with folded arms and downcast eyes, but they listen. Finally, we are confronted with weary eyes. Innovation? Oh, dear, it's second nature here! We launch new products on the market every year. We survey our customers regularly, ask them how satisfied they are and what they expect from us. And we even have an elaborate suggestion scheme. Fine, we could spruce that up a bit to get staff to put forward more improvements. But technologically, we lead the world and have done for years. So don't tell us anything about innovation. You are coming today from where we were yesterday ...

Typical. Typical engineer's mentality.

Typical. Typical engineer's mentality. All too often, sadly, innovation just means creating new products out of new technologies. Engineers and product developers run around trade fairs and cram together at technology congresses. And when they see the latest technical gadget, they get all excited. Brilliant technology! Oh, how absolutely brilliant! How can we incorporate that into our product? And then they storm off into their offices and laboratories and throw themselves into their work like Gyro Gearloose on speed.

Let's take the example of the Golf 5. Volkswagen was hell bent on integrating luxury-class technology into the compact class. The engineers thought that was a brilliant idea. So they gave this bog-standard car a multi-steering rear axle that was normally only used in the latest Mercedes-Benz or BMW. Then they waited for the applause that, sadly, never came. Even car testers from special-interest automotive magazines could find no significant difference in the way it handled compared with cars with a standard chassis. The more simply designed Opel Astra, for example, did just as well in comparative tests, and it was even classed as a slightly more sporty drive.

But if the difference is barely perceptible even to professionals, what use is this high-tech rear axle to granddad on his trips to the garden centre? None. Yet he still has to pay for the sophisticated design. No wonder Volkswagen lost market share because of excessive prices, and had to tempt customers with extras such as free climate control. At the expense of profitability, of course.

As long as engineers are arrogant enough to believe that their technology is just what the market needs, the products will fail.

The Golf's rear axle is an example of an innovation that isn't actually an innovation at all. Why not? Because the planning was out of synch with actual customer needs. This is a widespread disease, and not only in Germany. Koichi Tanaka, the Japanese Nobel laureate in chemistry for 2002, describes the phenomenon as tripping up because of failure to interpret the market correctly, making the mistake of taking technology too seriously and disregarding the needs of potential customers. In his opinion, as long as engineers are arrogant enough to believe that their technology is just what the market needs, the products will fail.

Of course, a company needs new products. And just as evidently, existing products have to be improved. We would never deny that. But that is never, n-e-v-e-r a substitute for real innovation. New products are innovative mostly when they surprise the customer by offering a value they have never experienced before. Something that drives engineers into paroxysms of enthusiasm may leave the customer cold.

The Gillette eight-blade syndrome: shaving with a Samurai sword might well be more practical.

We like to describe what we are currently seeing in many companies as the Gillette eight-blade syndrome. It all began in the 1960s with a twin-blade shaver. Fine, the idea was pretty good. But then nothing better occurred to Gillette than to bolt more and more blades on to its wet razors. First came blades number three and four, and now they've got to no fewer than six blades – five in front, one at the back. We will no doubt see number eight if we wait long enough. Shaving with a Samurai sword might well be more practical.

3 Es: events, experiences, emotions

When it comes to innovation, companies need to think about both the product and the customer experience. Yes, that's right: the customer experience! Okay, it's easier said than done. It is undoubtedly simpler for many companies to build real engineering performance into their products than to understand the customer's emotions. But Apple's iPod, for example, clearly demonstrates that engineering performance is very far from being the crucial factor at the product level these days. There are better MP3 players – technically speaking. But everybody wants the iPod, because it's the coolest. Well, why is that?

It's because of things that have absolutely nothing to do with the technology inside. First, the really cool design. IPods simply look phenomenal – minimalistic and unique. Second, the brilliant iTunes service. The MP3 players come with a matching website where the customer can download thousands and thousands of songs. This complementary innovation completes the deal. In this case, innovation is solid technology plus cool design plus unique service.

Innovation is when the customer gives three hearty cheers and reaches for his wallet. But when does he cheer, when does he reach for his wallet?

The measure of true innovation is actually simple: innovation is when the customer gives three hearty cheers and reaches for his wallet. Anything else is theoretical debate from the Alabama I.M. Neanderthal School for Advanced Management Studies. When we confront companies with this twin view of innovation – the product and the customer experience – the response is usually "Yes, that's true, actually". Basically so obvious, it has just never been seen that way. It was a blind spot. Steve Jobs and Apple have demonstrated how dangerous that can be for less innovative companies. Because with iTunes, Apple has revolutionized the entire music industry. Nothing will ever be the same again.

We can hear the familiar voices raised: that's all very fine and nice, let Apple take a piece of the music industry and sell a cute product to the youngsters – but we make furniture, pipelines, hydraulic pumps … it can't be done in our industry!

Even the purist bookcase was not invented by IKEA or by someone named Billy, although some people like to think so.

IKEA's success story shows that innovation doesn't depend on product novelty. Everything, absolutely everything that the Swedes sell to their customers pre-dates the company: tables, beds, chairs, sofas, lamps, wardrobes. Even the purist bookcase was not invented by IKEA or by someone named Billy, although some people like to think so.

At the product level, IKEA's innovation rate is and always has been minimal. Ingvar Kamprad, the company's founder, is only a billionaire today because he revolutionized the way people buy and use furniture. His product wasn't innovative, but his business model was. An important component is the catalogue. It has enjoyed cult status for years. With an annual circulation of 118 million copies in 23 languages, it is said to be the most read "book" after the Bible. In its cornucopia of brightly coloured pages, the IKEA philosophers communicate three values to humanity: multiculturalism, sociability and a love of children. He cooks, she sits at the computer, the children play on the sofa, but it has to involve cool furniture at a cool price. Somehow or other, you can't help feeling that the people shown there always wash their own coffee cups and cycle to work in an ecologically correct manner. He buys one shirt less every year – to reduce pesticides in cotton fields. She is constantly on her mobile phone, speaks Icelandic, Polish, Chinese, English and is serene and calm even over her seven o'clock muesli breakfast.

That's the world of IKEA: the future is uncertain as never before, so the home becomes the last bastion of love. The appropriate furnishings, designed by in-house staff, are produced cheaply and in large quantities by partner companies. If you visit IKEA at one of its green-field sites, you will find everything attractively set out up top, and a gigantic storage area below from which the self-assembly products can be packed straight into your tiny VW Polo (how are you supposed to get it all in?) and carted off home. At the end of the journey, the customer has the privilege of trying his skill as a furniture assembler with a minuscule Allen key.

This company controls the entire value chain. It integrates its customers as free labour and has ultimately succeeded through emotionalization in establishing itself as a cult brand, outside Sweden at least. Friends of minimalist design, price-conscious families and Sweden fans alike benefit from IKEA.

Know what the customer will want tomorrow

So it works with furniture as well. But even players who offer far simpler products can be innovative without changing anything about the product itself. One great example also comes from Scandinavia. Danish dairy company Arla has found a brilliant distribution model for a product as simple as milk that beats competitors on speed and freshness. Arla guarantees that the cows are milked every evening, the milk is bottled by midnight and is fresh in the shops the next morning. By this means, Arla has captured a 50 per cent market share in Denmark. The usual way to attempt to win customers would probably have been to offer ten new flavours – from kiwi to mango – and then add fourteen and a half different varieties of fat content. But Arla thought simply and brilliantly from the customer's point of view, and developed a much more sustainable innovation. That, in turn, is rewarded by the customers. They give three hearty cheers, get out their wallets and run to the checkout.

But how is a company to know in advance when the customer will give three hearty cheers, get out his wallet, and run? A lot of companies tell themselves: we'll just ask our customers. It's a bright enough idea in principle, but it can come back to haunt you. You have to know how to do it right.

Customers will only think a new, revolutionary, fantastic offer is fantastic once it is on the market ... and they no longer want the old product.

Customers have a tendency to stick to what they know. If you ask them what they want, the answer is simple: everything the way it has always been, but better and cheaper. Customers move within their own horizon of experience, within the familiar sphere. And the answers that market research delivers bear that out. That means: customers will only think a new, revolutionary, fantastic offer is fantastic once it is on the market ... and they no longer want the old product. Before that, no one will be able to tell you anything about a successful innovation. Hopefully, you'll then be making the new product, and not the old one that everybody loved only yesterday!

So companies have to get inventive themselves. Or do you reckon some customer came along and asked Steve Jobs to invent the iPod? Was 3M bombarded with petitions to create the Post-it? Does somebody call Nespresso and say "Hey, I would like you to invent the unique capsule system that provides fast, hassle-free brewing of gourmet coffee"?

Did some customer come along and ask Steve Jobs to invent the iPod?

Years ago, Ford wanted to build a car that would fulfil 100 per cent of its customers' wishes. Thousands and thousands of car owners were asked what they would expect of a new vehicle. When the market research results were analysed, engineers tried to meet the requirements exactly. The outcome was probably the most average, most boring car of all time. We don't even remember what it was called. Escordeo or Scorpionada or whatever. It had no character and triggered no emotions. It was the triumph of sub-mediocrity and a complete flop. No wonder – after all, it met the expectations of potential buyers 100 per cent. Big yawn.

Why do these things happen? You can literally feel it: out of fear! People want to minimize risk. They are afraid of swinging high with a bold idea and then falling flat on their faces. With the sweat of fear on their brows, they test new products for marketability until those products become deadly boring. But by doing that, they also avoid the "risk" of a megahit.

One company that knows what it's doing in this respect is Google. First of all, the employees do their job and think up exciting new products. But from a certain point onwards, as development boss Marissa Mayer knows only too well, it's impossible to tell what the customer will ultimately think of a new idea. The marketing department can discuss it for ever, but they're really just reading tea leaves.

And so Google puts its beta versions online for the customers. Web users can try various alternatives. The most popular one then becomes the final product.

Fear and innovation are like fire and water

Very simple, really. And yet many companies find it infinitely difficult to experiment even a little bit and take this kind of pragmatic approach. Why is that? Let's keep digging. The reasons lie deeper. It is simply a question of corporate culture. When talking about innovation, people in most companies will point the finger: there's the person responsible. Those people over there from the other section are the ones who develop new ideas. A lot of people still believe that the department with the nerdy, bespectacled scientists is responsible for innovations. Leave them to grub away at their research, and they'll put the greatest invention since sliced bread on the board's desk one day.

People also used to think that manufacturing needed a separate department responsible for quality. The "Quality Control department" did "quality management". But the Japanese still produced better quality at ever lower prices. Some time at the end of the 1980s, beginning of the 1990s, it dawned on most companies that quality was the responsibility of every, really every, member of staff. If you want to produce premium quality, then every employee has to internalize what "premium" means. Nowadays, that's taken for granted. For innovation, on the other hand, the process has just begun.

A lot of people still believe that the department with the nerdy, bespectacled scientists is responsible for innovations.

Today, knowledge is available all over the world. Hence, innovation is teamwork – or it doesn't happen. New knowledge arises when as many people as possible get together, exchange their knowledge and experience and put them back together again in a new way, often on the basis of conflicting ideas. The process has to be interdisciplinary, international, cross-generational and take place outside of hierarchical models.

We are indebted to German performance artist Joseph Beuys for the famous saying "Everyone is an artist". This statement shocked a bourgeois society for which art was the province of a superior caste of chosen people who appeared to have been introduced to the *Weltgeist* in person. This one-time revolutionary slogan can be applied to today's companies. Beuys goes business: everyone is an innovator. Today, everyone shares responsibility for ensuring his company's continuing success. Everyone can reinvent his job.

Beuys goes business: everyone is an innovator.

Of course, the boss can't just ask the workforce, "Hey, had any ground-breaking ideas today?" That's not how it works. And you can't transform a workforce into daring, inventive geniuses by decree. An innovation campaign printed on glossy paper and launched by the top management doesn't help much either. That kind of approach will make people pretend to be innovative – until the second the boss turns his back. If you want to transform all your staff into innovators, you not only have to communicate this intention clearly but you must also teach them how to become innovators.

Whirlpool, the American domestic appliances manufacturer, did just that. Throughout the company there are now more than 500 so-called innovation mentors. People can turn to them at any time with new ideas. They are not there to pat people on the back and distribute bonus cheques, but to review every idea and link it with other new ideas. They have received special training for that purpose. On top of that, all 15,000 employees have completed online courses about innovation, to enable them to appraise new ideas correctly themselves. Whirlpool is actually a dinosaur of the manufacturing race. But unlike those colossal reptiles, the company would like to continue its existence even under a radical climate change. Like today's.

Managers who fail to get the point make ideas a power issue.

Such "innovation mentoring" only works in an open corporate culture. Managers who fail to get the point make ideas a power issue. When that happens, the quality of an idea is irrelevant. The only thing that counts is who had it. And what if the best idea comes from a talented newcomer with no power base in the company? Obviously, the opportunity is thrown away, the idea is lost. And the talent generally doesn't stick around the company for long either. Clever companies, on the other hand, examine every idea minutely for its potential. Even if it comes from the janitor. That is the only way to handle ideas properly.

Get creative!

Because innovation can't be ordained from above, however, management can only try to create an environment in which this mindset comes as second nature. After all, "nature" is just what it is: all employees have ideas. That's quite normal, a result of day-on-day, intense engagement with a subject matter. No one can work on something long-term without having ideas about it. The question is simply: is it worth his while to tell anyone? Every employee is an innovator – unless he is stopped.

And every employee *has to* be an innovator. That's not metaphysics, but a survival technique. It's the only possibility nowadays; you have no other option! In a real-time, affluent society, a market player from San Diego, Moscow, Jakarta or Mumbai will copy your new product line, sometimes in a matter of weeks. You can complain about it, you can try to patent your ideas … but it won't help in the long run. There is no permanent protection against product imitation. Your only chance is to be on the market with a fresh, new idea while your competitors around the world are still in meetings, debating how to market the idea they've just swiped.

And every employee *has to* be an innovator. That's not metaphysics, but a survival technique.

Now, can't the well-oiled machine called "employee suggestion scheme" help you there? Surely they can produce a few brainwaves, can't they? It's a nice idea, but unfortunately there is one tiny snag: suggestion schemes have about as much to do with innovation as Bambi has to do with a real live stag.

Suggestion schemes are about improving the status quo, not about **21** creating genuine novelties. Employees put forward good ideas, and they are important, but as a rule they only affect their own immediate working environment and contribute mainly to saving costs. For example, they are about moving the VDU 30 centimetres to the right so that staff can pick up the telephone faster. That saves time and ultimately money, because the employee takes calls quicker and can therefore complete more of them per hour. The controllers then work out that this efficiency gain will lead to a saving of 10 eurocents per week per employee. At 100 employees, that would be as much as €5200 in 10 years. Wow!

Ideas to improve the status quo are good and important. All the same, good companies don't just have suggestion schemes, they have ideas. And they don't offer big rewards for every idea expressed by an employee. To us, reward systems are fatally reminiscent of training a seal to perform tricks. For every idea delivered per instructions, people are rewarded with a herring. The thought that employees have to be induced by incentives and rewards to have ideas and pass them on presents a dubious image of humanity. If no ideas are put forward in a company, it's not because the rewards are too low, but because there's something wrong with the leadership culture.

Good companies don't just have suggestion schemes, they have ideas.

And not even a sophisticated incentive system will change that – it will even make the problem worse, because yesterday's rewards are today's norm and tomorrow's vested right. And these rights grow. Employees aren't stupid. Why should they give away something for free if they can get money for it? That's human nature. Sooner or later, it carries every incentive system to absurd conclusions. So abolish the rewards! Your employees are not seals. Innovations can be neither ordained nor purchased.

Yesterday's rewards are today's norm and tomorrow's vested right.

Fuel the innovation pipeline

Google's 70–20–10 formula for innovation shows that incentives do not have to be monetary in order to work. The ideal target for the Internet company's technical people is to spend 70 per cent of their working hours on ongoing projects, to learn and to think about new possibilities 20 per cent of the time and devote 10 per cent of their paid working hours to far-out ideas.

The 20 per cent is where the most interesting projects emerge. In other words, if you want to fuel the innovation pipeline, inject a bit of personal freedom into the process.

CHAPTER 3

BUSINESS UNCONVENTIONALISM: THE COOL IDEAS AREN'T TO BE FOUND IN YOUR OWN INDUSTRY

We were doing a consulting project for a traditional German business: heavy industry, coal and steel, roots in the 19th century. And – take note – the invitation came from a woman. She was one of the few female top managers in this industrial group, had known us for some time, and invited us to participate in the annual strategy meeting. As two critical minds with an external viewpoint, we were to challenge them and contribute new ideas. It was the first time that externals had taken part in such a meeting.

The decision to invite two externals was taken only because the first stirrings of unease were being felt in this conglomerate, spoiled by fifty years of post-war success. Though the figures still looked good, they could see difficult times ahead. In the briefing before the meeting, one manager had lamented falling margins, new competitors from Eastern Europe and Asia, and disloyal customers. Finally, they had sent us a paper outlining their strategy as preparatory material. This included 48 nicely designed PowerPoint slides that would give us an insight into the internal workings of the Group. "You'll be able to see how we see ourselves," we were told on the phone.

Benchmarking or best practices: never anything but a threadbare attempt to disguise your own lack of ideas.

After we had battled our way through all the bar charts, columns of figures and lofty words, one thing was crystal clear: this strategy was so bland that it would have worked for any player in their industry. Change the logo – abracadabra, its key competitor would have been quite happy to claim it for its own. It was as if they had taken the most pleasing terms from a set of linguistic building blocks and put them together. We decided it was time to take off the velvet gloves and confront the managers openly with this fact at the meeting.

Step one: accept the bitter truth

"This is all very plausible and nice," we told them. "Satisfy customers, improve internal communication, make better use of resources, add new services. Yes, of course, super. Now, please show us one single company in your industry that says 'We will kick our customers up the bottom and we don't give a cuss about internal communication.' We are one hundred per cent certain that your competitors have exactly the same papers. Send it to them by email, and they'll say: 'Hey, that's our new strategy paper'. These are extremely cautious me-too strategies wrapped in lukewarm platitudes. They won't get you very far. You'll make progress if you have the answers to questions like: what makes us unique? And what is our *unique value* to our customers? The one our competitors couldn't imitate in two seconds flat? Everything depends on the answers to these questions."

But let's take a look around. We can't help getting the feeling that a lot of companies don't waste too much time thinking about these questions. Instead, they copy what is successful elsewhere. Naturally, it isn't called copying. No, there are much nicer words for it: benchmarking, for example, or best practices. But whatever you call it, it's never anything but a threadbare attempt to disguise your own lack of ideas. And so entire industries dwindle into karaoke clubs where everyone sings someone else's song.

That's legitimate up to a point – but it should never be allowed to become the over-arching strategy. In today's saturated, tired markets, offering products that are barely distinguishable from those of your competitors is business suicide. Customers are already drowning in a flood of me-too products; they are swimming in a sea of sameness.

Abnormality, un-normality, anti-normality, trans-normality conquer markets.

If you offer a "standard" product that is quite okay, you've lost before you ever start. Even if here and there it is 1.75 per cent better than the competitors' product. Quite okay is clinically dead. The watchword is d-i-f-f-e-r-e-n-t. Abnormality, un-normality, anti-normality, trans-normality conquer markets. And you don't do it by looking sideways at the competition.

Instead, you always have to keep two balls in the air at the same time: uniqueness and excellent value to the customer. Amazon can do it, CNN – the first 24-hour news broadcaster – and eBay and IKEA can do it. None of them grew out of a me-too strategy; they all dared to be different. They created a temporary monopoly for themselves. They are one step ahead when competitors are still toiling to imitate the original concept. The company that only ever observes competitors in its own industry will never do anything but run along behind them.

What can an automotive engineer learn from a lifestyle broadcaster?

But how can you liberate yourself from competing in a sea of sameness? Open your eyes! Open your eyes and look away from your own company and its immediate competitors! That is part of what we mean by "unconventional thinking". For example, a bank might take a look at the automotive industry. It sees that a certain car is available in the "Classic", "Elegance" and "Avantgarde" product lines, with different features. And then it wonders: couldn't we have accounts in the "Classic", "Elegance" and "Avantgarde" product lines, with different features?

Such ideas often sound out of the ordinary to begin with. Of course they do; they are anything but ordinary. But the most frequent reaction to them is rejection: "No one else is doing that, and our customers will think that this idea is ridiculous." People laugh initially, because the idea sounds a bit crazy. But if you set yourself the goal of creating something new and unique, you have to do something that everyone may initially laugh at or shake their heads over – in a way, that's the test. If everyone nods agreement and says: "Yes, that makes sense," there may be a dozen competitors already doing it.

If you set yourself the goal of creating something new and unique, you have to do something that everyone may initially laugh at – in a way, that's the test.

Let's take another example. This is something we find so irritating that we are not only going to mention it here but will have to repeat it in Chapter 10. No, no, you don't have to skip forward right now. It's this: we travel a lot. And on almost every trip we get annoyed because we always have to check out of hotels by twelve o'clock at the latest. A cast-iron and utterly senseless law of the hotel industry. They must be learning at hotel management school that that's the way it is. But if we arrive at an airport at 9 p.m. and rent a car from Sixt or Avis, we don't have to give it back the next day at 12 noon. And hotels have an immense advantage over car rental companies: rooms do not move. How often do you check into a hotel in Munich and want to drop the room off in Hanover the next day?

The thinking behind the twelve o'clock rule is completely out of line with guests' needs, isn't it? But when you discuss it with hoteliers, it's like talking to frogs about draining the pond. The twelve o'clock rule is a law. Period. End of story. Basta. Amen.

Why don't hotels take an example from the car rental companies, and give guests a room for 24 hours? It's that dratted industry mentality. "That's how we've always done it." They act as if Moses had come down from Mount Sinai with an 11th Commandment on his tablets.

Outsiders make better revolutionaries

That's why outsiders and newcomers are typically the ones to shake up established industries. They don't give a cuss about industry norms. By outsiders, we don't mean the type of office lunatics whose strange clothing and odd social behaviour indicate congenital or acquired weaknesses in their cerebral constitution, as superficial analyses in office corridors generally point out. We mean people who look at existing markets and target groups from an impartial, external point of view and then do something courageous: they reinvent the business. A fantastic example of this is Klaus Heymann, who, with his Naxos label, started to stir up the market for classical CDs in the year 1987. His success made such massive waves that the whole market for classical music was transformed and rejuvenated. Heymann was and is an unconventional thinker par excellence.

Do you remember the way classical music CDs looked in the mid-1980s? Smooth and perfect; glossy photos in muted colours showing pictures of star conductors – Karajan, Bernstein, Muti – defined their image. And always in combination with the world's major orchestras: Berlin and Vienna, Amsterdam, the big five from the USA. And of course top conductors and major orchestras cost a lot of money. That meant that no CD of reasonably recent production was to be had below a price of €15. The seemingly winning combination consisted of stars, media hype, high gloss and high prices.

And then along came Klaus Heymann, a German businessman who had been quick to seize the opportunities of the business boom in the Far East. From his base in the then British colony of Hong Kong he started to revolutionize the classics market. And by the way, Heymann was not some poor little soul from a direct sales team for vacuum cleaners who was struck by his entrepreneurial vision, including business plan and financing model, as by lightning out of the blue when plodding from house to house. Heymann approached his entrepreneurial vision step by step and with careful planning, starting with some fundamental questions: does the classic CD actually have to cost €15? Does it take world stars to play Brahms's Third Symphony when there are superbly trained musicians all over the world, particularly in Eastern Europe? Are marketing budgets the size of Portugal's gross domestic product needed to sell the classics? No, was Heymann's answer. There are other ways.

So the German created the Naxos label, working from Hong Kong. Right from the start, the CDs had a simple but unmistakable design: instead of expensive photos of artists, the covers were decorated with old woodcuts for which no licence fees were payable. Instead of stars, they featured musicians like Cappella Istropolitana from the Slovakian city of Bratislava, which at that time was still behind the Iron Curtain. But above all: each CD cost less than €5. So – not €13.50 instead of €15. No. €5. One third of the usual price.

Hardly were the first CDs on the shelves when the retailers were banging on Heymann's doors for more. The interesting thing was that Naxos attracted entirely new customer segments. At that price, even die-hard Depeche Mode fans were curious to find out what this Beethoven guy's sound was like. Naxos went on to produce CDs for beginners. Classics for dreamers, classics for lovers, classics for dinner were a culture shock at the time – and sensationally successful.

At that price, even die-hard Depeche Mode fans were curious to find out what this Beethoven guy's sound was like.

And what did the competitors do? They laughed at him. They simply didn't take this guy out in Hong Kong seriously, and were taking bets that he would soon vanish from the scene. Sadly for them, that didn't happen, so they tried to wipe Naxos out. When that didn't work either, the music industry started to copy Naxos. What a compliment! Universal, EMI et al. launched their own cheap labels. But Naxos's lead, its temporary monopoly, was enough to enable it to take the next step forward.

While competitors were treating customers to ancient recordings from the 1960s, Naxos focused in the 1990s more and more on quality: current recordings, exciting young artists and an ever widening repertoire. Bach and Brahms were joined by Ligeti and Henze – and found buyers who would never previously have bought contemporary serious music. In 1995, Naxos was voted Label of the Year in Cannes. Today, it has its own shelf in the Berlin media department store Dussmann, separately labelled just as are the "Opera" or "New" sections. And now, it is not just musicians from Bratislava who fight for this label's recording contracts. Naxos is like a blueprint for business unconventionalism. Klaus Heymann was not an industry insider – and that was precisely his advantage. His objective was never to follow the example of brain-dead CEOs who respectfully observe existing conventions. Quite the contrary: he was not at all fussed about the unwritten rules of the industry. That was the secret of his success. That, and a good dollop of boldness and persistence.

Klaus Heymann was not an industry insider – and that was precisely his advantage.

Which puts him in excellent company. The late Anita Roddick, the inventor of the cosmetics outlet chain The Body Shop, also swept aside the cast-iron laws of the cosmetics industry. The Body Shop's aim was not just to be better, but above all to be different. And when Richard Branson entered the airline industry, it was not with a desire to copy British Airways. Virgin Atlantic would simply be different. It would be rock 'n' roll to take off by.

Good ideas are super. But they are only half the battle.

It was clear to all these unconventionalists that once the establishment had stopped laughing, it would try to destroy them. But they were not afraid of confrontation. We cannot emphasize strongly enough how important that is. Good ideas are super. But they are only half the battle. We then also have to be prepared to implement them and keep on implementing them. And we cannot give in timidly at the first sign of intimidation by established competitors. Austrian economist Joseph Schumpeter described this attitude along these lines: an entrepreneur really only becomes an entrepreneur when he does something apparently against the grain of the majority, the apparently immovable economic and social "truth", because he believes in his idea and implements it obstinately. The idea is less important than the ability to stand by it.

Obviously, outsiders and newcomers have it easier here. They have not had any unwritten laws of an industry rammed into them during their training. They don't gibber with respect when faced with an industry's alpha males.

Industry insiders can be flexible, too – if they are doing badly enough

Many examples show that it is easier for outsiders to reinvent an industry, because they do not carry the burden of too much industry knowledge. Nevertheless, there are also examples of where change started from the inside of an industry. Have you heard of Zespri Gold? For those of you who don't frequent greengrocers' stalls, here is the explanation: it's a kiwi fruit with yellow flesh. And this fruit is patented. Yes, exactly, just like electric motors or can openers are patented in other industries. Patented fruit? You may think it's completely idiotic – or brilliant. And this is how it happened: since the 1970s, New Zealand farmers have bestowed on us the blessing of the kiwi. The fruit rapidly became so popular in Europe and North America that Italian, Spanish and South African farmers also cultivated it. The customer saw no reason why this fruit necessarily had to come from New Zealand, and bought anything that was round, brown and fuzzy on the outside and green on the inside.

Patented fruit? You may think it's completely idiotic – or brilliant.

Now, the New Zealand farmers could have appealed to the politicians and demanded protectionist measures in the face of falling market shares. Instead, they sought a solution by looking beyond the borders of their industry. As a result, they developed a very clever product innovation – a new and patent-protected fruit! All 2,500 New Zealand kiwi farmers united to form Zespri International Ltd and, together with the state-owned Fruit Science Institute, they developed a new kiwi which came on the market in the year 2000 under the name of Zespri Gold. It has a golden yellow centre and a sweet flavour reminiscent of tropical fruit. In the year 2005, sales were just under €150 million. By 2009, the New Zealanders (themselves traditionally nicknamed "Kiwis" in English-speaking countries) aim to reach the €650 million mark. And the clever trick is that kiwi farmers from other countries who would like to get a slice of the Zespri's success have to pay licence fees to New Zealand's farmers. Zespri International Ltd has now concluded lucrative licensing agreements with fruit plantations in Italy, France, Japan, Korea, Chile and the USA.

The clever Kiwis from New Zealand have learnt their lesson: they invest €6 million a year into quality improvements, research into new varieties and environmentally friendly production methods. A new patent-protected fruit is already in the innovation pipeline: a kiwi with blood-red flesh. So unconventional thinkers exist within industries, too. It's just a shame that way too often the water has to be up to most people's necks before they will budge.

And yet, innovation can be fun. Reinventing, looking beyond industry boundaries and developing innovative product and service concepts are among the most exciting things you can do in your life. We do not know any innovators who are not passionate about their subject. Many of them don't just want to do business, but also improve the world a little. And some of them manage to do it, too.

Many of them don't just want to do business, but also improve the world a little. And some of them manage to do it, too.

Take Indian ophthalmologist Govindappa Venkataswamy, for example. In his country 21 million people suffer from cataract. A few short decades ago, hardly anyone could afford an operation. And then the ophthalmologist, now 87 years old, looked over the rim of his guild's spectacles. And his gaze fell on – McDonald's. It wasn't so much the Big Macs and French fries that attracted him, but more the idea of standardization and licensing. How would it be, thought Dr V, as he is known to his admirers, if we were to adopt the idea of standardized processes, enabling us to treat thousands of patients a year?

Today, Dr V and his medical practitioners perform perfect and highly efficient surgery on 230,000 patients per annum. Only one third of them has to pay anything. Most are treated free of charge because they are poor. Nevertheless, Dr V's chain of hospitals has a turnover of US$10 million per annum. The figures are of secondary importance, however. With his idea, Venkataswamy has made a modest contribution to making the world a better place, the trail of a small comet leaving its mark on the universe. It is not given to all of us to be a Dr V. But we all have the chance to at least *try*.

CHAPTER 4

CHANGING PLAYING FIELDS: CREATING NEW MARKETS IS MORE LUCRATIVE THAN WRINGING THE LAST DROP OUT OF OLD ONES

We are now going to talk about PVC. Get ready … we once met a manufacturer from a mid-sized German PVC company. The company produces PVC sections. The PVC sections are needed by manufacturers of PVC windows. They put PVC sections together to make PVC windows. It follows that PVC window manufacturers are the customers of a PVC sections manufacturer. Their growth opportunities depend on the market for PVC windows. And the competitors of a PVC section manufacturer are other PVC section manufacturers, who in turn supply manufacturers of PVC windows, who make PVC windows out of them. Seems a fair assumption. The company in question thought so for many years.

And now let's talk about innovation. Get set, go! One day, the head of this company spotted a name he didn't know in his customer files. This customer was not buying huge volumes of PVC sections, but had obviously been ordering them regularly for some time. The company name didn't sound like a new manufacturer of PVC windows. The boss decided to do a Web search on this customer. He could hardly believe his eyes: it was an advertising agency. Is the downturn in advertising so bad that they're going into the PVC windows business now? he asked himself. Are they welding windows together in their spare time?

The boss couldn't get it out of his head, so he decided to ask the advertising agency what they were doing with the PVC sections. It turned out that the advertising guys were cutting the sections into pieces and putting them together to make advertising displays. The people at the agency loved the material: weatherproof, very sturdy, lightweight and it could be used again and again.

It's easy money, because the company has succeeded in establishing a temporary monopoly.

Wait a minute, thought the boss. We could supply them with the right parts for their advertising displays to start with! They sat down together with the agency and developed the right sections.

The logical next step was for the PVC company's salesmen to start cold calling other advertising agencies. And they were successful. More and more agencies were thrilled by these innovative, flexible components for advertising displays. Nowadays, advertising agencies account for 10 per cent of the PVC manufacturers' revenues. It's not a huge sum, but it's easy money, because the company has succeeded in establishing a temporary monopoly. Instead of entering into cutthroat price competition with other section-makers, it simply looked for new customers.

Leave the pie to the others; the pie shop is more interesting ...

What the example of the PVC manufacturer teaches us is that if you want to grow, you have to cross lines. You have to actively develop entirely new customer groups. You don't need to do it aggressively, you have to be cleverer. You don't need to work harder, you just have to think more.

If you want to grow, you have to cross lines.

Unfortunately, most companies still think of a market as a big pie. A pie with everybody fighting for the biggest piece day on day. But because everyone wants the same thing, they get involved in bitter rivalries for customer segments, competitive advantages and market shares. Yet it's clear to anyone with a teaspoonful of common sense that it's nonsense to beat each other up for something that already exists if you can create something new instead.

We suggest you stop wasting all your energy fighting for the biggest piece of pie. Just bake a pie of your own! And if it doesn't come out right first time, then at least make a delicious, melt-in-the-mouth muffin. Like our PVC manufacturer with his lucrative sideline.

To put it in plain terms: of course, product and service innovations are very important. But that's not the end of the story. When the products change, the customer structures change automatically with them. So you have to keep on thinking about how to develop new customer groups. Customers that nobody in your own industry has ever thought about.

Customers to whom you can sell unique products and services in a unique way. Every so often in the history of business over the last 20 years you will find companies that have broken their industry's game rules and opened up entirely new customer groups with fresh market offerings. That's why we would like to get a bit physical with you at this point. The two examples discussed below show that there are no excuses for the status quo – in any industry.

First of all, there is the concept developed by Swiss national Werner Kieser. He wondered how new customer groups could be attracted to fitness studios. He deliberately discarded the kind of customers who panic because they still haven't exercised themselves into the *Men's Health* ISO 9000 standard six-pack after numerous visits to the gym. Kieser thought up a completely new concept, which he called health-oriented strength training. His starting point was one of the most widespread popular ailments: "a strong back knows no pain" became Kieser Training's claim. The man from Switzerland created an entirely unique corporate identity. His fitness studios are ascetic, lean, even of a Calvinist severity. No juice bar, no sauna, no aerobics or Pilates class, no cardio equipment. Just you and machines that build up supporting muscle. Kieser addresses a target group that doesn't exist in the same form in any other studio. The typical Kieser customer is 44 years old, not particularly sporty, and has no relevant experience in fitness: 80 per cent of customers had never been in a health club before they came to Kieser Training. To put it another way: these customers had never gone to a fitness studio of the normal type.

Kieser Training is successful. Because it's different. Thanks to his unique clientele, Kieser is hardly in competition with other studios. He has succeeded in establishing a temporary monopoly, not by reinventing the fitness studio as such, but by asking who the "typical" fitness studio customers were, and what offerings were used to attract them, before systematically challenging the status quo and boldly going in a new direction.

Extended competition: the real playing field extends beyond the boundary line

The first step towards such a strategy is always to ask yourself who your competitors really are. Most companies define their competition far too narrowly. Recently, one of us was invited to an innovation award ceremony in Austria. Medium-sized companies were well represented, all of them making serious efforts to be innovative and go new ways. Chatting to these entrepreneurs, however, soon revealed that almost without exception they regarded peers from the same industry as their competitors. However, the competitive arena is much larger than that.

In this day and age, competition is primarily about attention and time. Customers give their attention to the product and the company that they find attractive. Emotional resonance is converted directly into attention. And the customer devotes most time to the provider with which he feels most comfortable. Even though a lot of companies don't want to believe it: customers will always compare apples with pears in this regard. Dissatisfaction with their bank is stored in the same place in the brain as satisfaction with a certain hotel they recently stayed at.

Creating new markets and setting your sights on new customers first means arriving at the most flexible possible definition of your own business. Nevertheless, most of the companies we know follow a fairly narrow groove. They just define themselves by what they do, in other words their products and services. They will say: "We make baked goods." And then they muster up what they have available to them for that purpose. For example: "We own three fully automated bakery lines in Hanover, Nuremberg and Graz." Instead of that, however, they could define themselves on the basis of their true core competence. That would sound totally different: "We offer people the opportunity to reward themselves from time to time in their everyday lives." Then, they will immediately see that they are not just in competition with other large bakeries with their Danish pastries and sticky buns. They are also competing with ice-cream vendors or coffee bars, in short: anything that allows the customer to purchase an inexpensive little treat in between times. And if the odd coffee bar manages to combine the sale of an espresso with a special atmospheric quality, it might certainly give the bakery chain with its dreary shop design something to think about. Even if all other bakeries look just the same and attract exactly the same customers.

The art of making a circus nightclub out of a hippy caravan

Our second example of a company that really understands how to open up completely new customer segments is the Cirque du Soleil. On one of our last trips to our old home, Phoenix, Arizona, an excursion to Las Vegas had to be on the itinerary. We love this glittering metropolis in the Nevada Desert, the world capital of entertainment. Naturally, we also took in the Cirque du Soleil. And it was fantastic! It's hard to believe that a company that stages superlative shows every evening around the globe was founded by a handful of Canadian hippies. And even to this day, Cirque du Soleil is no ordinary company.

"What am I going to do today that actually seems impossible?"

Company boss Daniel Lamarre once said something in an interview which underpins that thesis: "My typical office day starts with my asking myself: What am I going to do today that actually seems impossible?" Wow! Unfortunately, we know a lot of people who are more inclined to start their working day by saying something like: "How long before Friday afternoon comes round again?"

At Cirque du Soleil, the enthusiasm is almost tangible and infects the visitor straight away. Canada's hit cultural export has its roots in the year 1984, when the afore-mentioned hippies from Quebec got together to earn enough money for a modest living in the least bourgeois way possible. Today, that aspiration has grown into a globe-spanning entertainment machine with an annual turnover of $600 million. And please note: that's in the recession-plagued entertainment industry, where others are bemoaning falling demand and audiences' high price sensitivity.

So what did Cirque du Soleil actually do? Nothing less than completely reinvent the circus. And above all, entice people into circus shows who would normally never dream of going to one. That said, the term "circus" applies to Cirque du Soleil about as much as the term "dance band" fits the Rolling Stones. Musty tents, dusty floors, hard benches, dull animal numbers and moderately amusing clowns – Cirque du Soleil has none of these. Instead of aiming first and foremost at families as customers, the Cirque also targets adults and corporate customers. Cirque du Soleil does not compete with other circuses, but with the theatre, opera, cinema, restaurants and nightclubs. Both the show and the atmosphere are correspondingly high level. For example, there are no individual circus numbers, but a fully staged story, just like in a play or an opera. Companies holding incentive events or rewarding their best customers, as well as private individuals, buy tickets for several times the price they would be prepared to pay at a traditional circus box office.

But the company's real coup is multiplication. Every show is rehearsed by several ensembles, so that they can go on tour simultaneously. Twenty casting agents constantly tour the world to recruit acts. At the end of the day, Olympic gold medal winners like the Azerbaijani archer in "O" are just as much part of the deal as the snake girl from the Indian peasant circus. In addition to perfect training, Cirque du Soleil demands expression and spontaneity. Artists who fail to understand that will soar out of the door instead of through the air.

Positioning: a standpoint that makes growth possible

Cirque du Soleil has succeeded in becoming a global brand. According to Interbrand, it ranks 22nd, which puts it even above Disney. Not bad for a few ageing hippies. At the same time, the company's costs are going down through multiplication, though never at the expense of creativity. Seventy per cent of income goes back into new projects. To quote Daniel Lamarre again: "Our brand means creativity, and we can't neglect that." Audiences from New York to Moscow and at the permanently sold-out show in Las Vegas allow themselves to be drawn into sophisticated dream worlds, and are happy to pay €150 for the privilege. Cirque du Soleil re-captivates spectators who would previously have associated circuses with a few pleasant childhood memories at best.

Economists call monopolies "market failure".

So it does work. You can escape ruinous head-on-head competition by creating new markets that are distinctly different from the ones you served in the past. By leaving your previous competition behind – temporarily, at least. And by creating a quasi-monopoly for yourself through unconventional thinking. Economists call monopolies "market failure". For unconventionalists who are anything but ordinary, they mean a damn good business model. And Las Vegas has been the scene of huge value creation for quite some time, without producing anything in the classic industrial sense. People flood into the city because they are offered unique experiences.

The name Las Vegas came up recently in a public discussion here in Germany. Berlin-based star architect Hans Kollhoff tabled Las Vegas in an interview as a model for the economic development of the debt-ridden German capital. His reward was to be slated in much of the media. Of course, Kollhoff doesn't want to have Siegfried & Roy appear at the German Bundestag or to plaster the Kurfürstendamm with gambling casinos. He only meant to illustrate that an almost entirely deindustrialized big city in an isolated location with no important harbour or air cargo hub, and with only a few corporate head offices and large banks, can see its situation as an opportunity as well as a threat. Las Vegas is even in the middle of the desert – and it's booming! Berlin could ask itself how it can offer visitors outstanding experiences on the basis of its unique mixture of history, politics, arts, shopping and subcultures. After all, a second industrial revolution with a new Werner von Siemens and resurrected Emil Rathenau is an unlikely scenario.

But Germany offers positive examples, too. Hans-Peter Wodarz, for example, may not be quite as successful as Daniel Lamarre, but he has breathed new life into the restaurant trade with his shows "Pomp, Duck and Circumstance" and, most recently, "Belle et Fou". Basically, all he is doing is selling a dinner for more than €100 to people who would probably never enter a starred restaurant. But because he combines the meal with a unique show, people flock to his place – while other chefs and restaurateurs still believe that their main competition is the other restaurant around the corner. Yet before going out to eat, the customer will have decided against the cinema, a DVD, shopping, the theatre, cooking at home and many other options, so Wodarz's offering makes complete sense. Once you understand that, you will also succeed in taking the second step of changing your playing field.

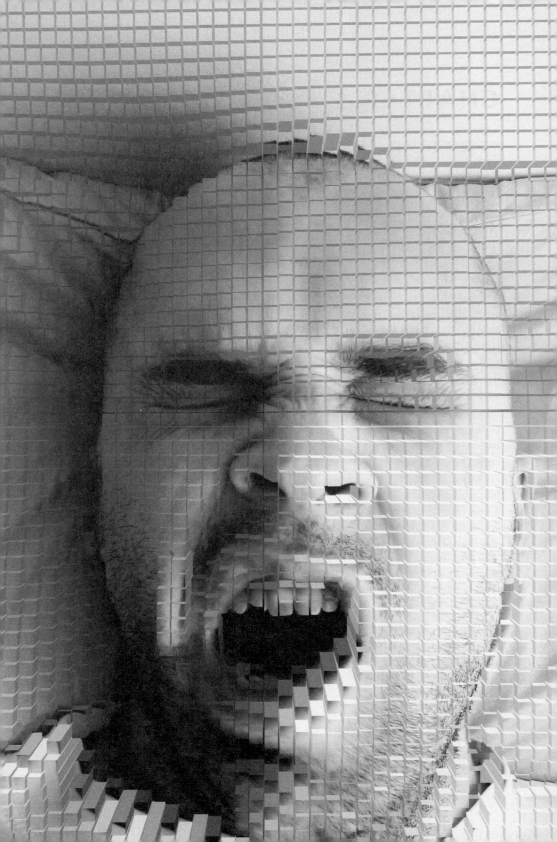

CHAPTER 5

BIG YAWN: THE BEST MINDS DON'T WORK FOR THE MOST BORING COMPANIES

When one of us was still teaching International Management at the Vienna University of Economics and Business Administration (WU Wien), he regularly invited practitioners as guest speakers, so that the students would get some vague notion of what was waiting for them out in the real world after graduation. On one occasion, a director from a large, newly privatized organization took to the lectern. The beautifully turned-out gentleman *d'un certain age* in the made-to-measure suit had been talking for over an hour, praising his former state-run conglomerate from every angle, and finally got round to the company's fantastic – in his eyes – trainee programme. Then he suddenly had the bright idea of asking the students directly: "Which of you would be interested in applying for our trainee programme?"

A deathly hush fell on the room. The students stared at their notes, at the ceiling, trying to avoid his gaze. No one evinced even the smallest trace of interest. It was unspeakably embarrassing. Even the faculty member-cum-host whose duty it was to save the situation needed a few agonizingly long seconds to find the right words to usher this top manager out circumspectly without giving him the impression that he had fallen flat on his face. Once he was safely ensconced in the back of his luxury limousine and the chauffeur was carrying him back to his office, the students remarked that they would rather die than work in the company he represented.

Why was that? How did this reaction come about? It has to be said, in all fairness, that our speaker had not made any stupid or embarrassing mistakes. On the contrary: apart from the excruciating self-praise, it was a very respectable speech. He had not let fall anything off-putting or scary about his company's management or staff. And besides, the students had no way of knowing what the inside of his company was really like, or whether the trainee programme was actually any good or not. Nevertheless, they didn't want to work for the company at any price. Their gut feeling just told them "never, ever!"

What attracts a bee to a flower?

With hindsight, the reason is entirely clear to us. The director hadn't said anything bad about his company – but nor had he said anything that would have made it attractive to the students. He was talking to gifted young people, but he didn't appeal to them at all. The idea of serving out their future careers in this company had no sex appeal. The man had made his company as appetizing as lukewarm, non-alcoholic beer in a teacup. This old-school executive, hankie tucked into his top pocket, cufflinks in his shirt sleeves, was a good reflection of his company – rock solid, but just boring. There were no bad vibrations coming from him, but, sadly, no good vibrations either.

And you know what? The students were right. We got better acquainted with the company later on: the hierarchical levels were cast in concrete, and the employees hung up their creativity, personal initiative and élan every morning on three hooks just behind the entrance door. For talents, an absolute desert. A lot has changed there now. But at that time, we just asked ourselves: who on earth would want to work here?

Who would *want to*. That is precisely the point. "Want to". Not "have to". Because the last few years have seen a 180-degree turnaround in the employment market for top talents. There was a time when companies could pick and choose. If you had a good degree and seemed well behaved and docile at the interview, you were graciously awarded a job. Nowadays, the employees pick and choose their companies. We are not talking about the low-wage sector or about easy, routine jobs – we should emphasize that at this point. In those sectors, jobseekers are still fighting over far too few offers. We are talking about the best minds, the new creative class, the guarantors of value creation. These high potentials no longer need to work for the Back of Beyond Utility Company when Google or BMW will take them on.

Nowadays, the employees are the ones who pick and choose.

Before you start thinking we are out of our minds, let us take a look across the ocean at California. Silicon Valley has led the way in this regard for years. It is a magnet for talented people who are prepared to work. And also for creative, unconventional thinkers and highly intelligent freaks of all kinds. The CEOs, in turn, do everything in their power to attract these talents. They try to achieve pop star status and win their potential employees as fans before the latter even put pen to their first application. And companies go to considerable lengths to be able to offer their best minds a top-class working environment.

First things first – people!

The magnet attracts the metal, not the other way round. And your company has to make itself into a talent magnet. Many companies still haven't geared their strategies rigorously enough to this situation. The trend, however, is inexorable. Not just in Silicon Valley, but everywhere. What priority do employees have in a corporate strategy? Is the notion "employees are our real assets" more than mere lip service? Sometimes the little things give the deepest insights. In the same way as unpolished shoes that don't go with an expensive suit. Visit the website of the drugstore chain Schlecker and call up the "Corporate principles" page. "Mobilize the initiative and contributions of the staff" is stated as one of the goals. That's all very fine and dandy. But what position does it hold in the corporate guidelines? First comes "sourcing policy", then "sales policy", then "customer policy", then "public relations work", and then – no, not the "employees", but the "personnel and organizational policy". Greater emotional distance would scarcely be possible. They don't talk about people, but about personnel: the faceless mass that adapts itself to the company's needs.

Personnel: the faceless mass that adapts itself to the company's needs.

Germany's dm drugstore chain sells almost exactly the same products as Schlecker. Its website is a total contrast. The second of its three "corporate principles" is: "to offer the people who work with us an environment where he/she can recognise and live their full potential". And the "dm customer principles" are immediately followed by the "dm employee principles". Could it be that a different spirit prevails here? The people at the dm drugstore chain are considered real assets, which has not been such a conspicuous feature of Schlecker in the past. dm's claim is "I'm treated as a human being here, so this is where I'll shop", while Schlecker proclaims itself as "modern and famous for its prices". Well, yeah, the prices are nice. What about the people side?

Clever organizations are magnets. They attract the best minds. People pick organizations where they feel comfortable and can grow as people. After all, they spend a good portion of their lives at the workplace. When asked by journalists, employees of dm drugstore chain consistently say that they've had lots of experience in other retailing companies, but they don't want to leave this company.

And what does the company have to gain from this? The customer? The investor? E-v-e-r-y-t-h-i-n-g! Because the employees *are* the company. If a company wants to be innovative and keep developing, it needs employees who embrace change. Who love innovation because they enjoy shaping their environment. We finally have to get it into our heads that employees are not an ingredient in an "organizational policy" but everything a company has. A-b-s-o-l-u-t-e-l-y everything!

When you go to the dentist, do you tell him where to place the drill?

It is sheer idiocy to hire intelligent people and then tell them what they have to do. When companies hire creative minds, they are bringing the power of innovation into the organization. But that power has to be allowed to develop. People need an environment where they can develop their full potential. And this in turn requires scope for development and trust. When you go to the dentist, do you tell him where to place the drill?

Attractions, not chains!

Let's take a football team as a comparison. We're not talking here about the third division, but a top club like Chelsea or Real Madrid. It's every talented youngster's dream to play for them one day. But would the managers of Bayern Munich or Madrid talk about their players as "employees", "the workforce", "staff", or even "human resources"? No! Instead, they will use expressions of esteem like "our players", "talents", "playmakers". After all, the players could sign a contract elsewhere at any time. In football it is understood that the players are the team, that they are the drivers of the club's success. Why isn't it the same in business?

Or imagine if the conductor of the Berlin Philharmonic Orchestra were to give a lecture at a music college and, at the end, ask the students: "which of you would be interested in playing in our orchestra?" I beg your pardon?

The students would quite rightly think it was a joke. Obviously, there is no doubt that a music student would like to play in one of the best orchestras in the world. The Berlin or Vienna Philharmonic, the Royal Concertgebouw Orchestra in Amsterdam and other leading orchestras exert such an attraction for musicians that they really don't have to worry about shrinking to the size of chamber ensembles in the years to come.

Being condemned for life to permanent employment in office cells in exchange for loyalty and obedience is no longer an option.

A third comparison: as authors, we are naturally confronted with the question of which publisher we want for a certain book. We aren't applying for a job; we select the publisher that suits us and that particular book best. Of course, the chemistry has to be right as well. We look at the other authors published by the company. Do we want to appear in the same series as them? Conversely, publishing houses are in competition with other publishers for bestselling authors that several publishers would love to have on board. The point is that the cards are reshuffled every time for every new book project. A different publisher may be the better choice for the author next time. Or a different author for the publisher, of course.

That principle applies to all companies: being condemned for life to permanent employment with shared accommodation in office cells in exchange for loyalty and obedience is no longer an option. Companies where work is a grey activity meandering slowly through grey buildings, and where grey managers rule over equally grey subordinates – that doesn't work nowadays. In any case, it is doubtful whether it was ever actually a good deal. Today, we are seeing more and more companies organizing around projects. That means they seek and find the best minds for a particular job. Over and over again. Companies like Cisco, SAP or BMW are already built to a large extent on such project-based structures. And, typically, they are also among the companies that exert the greatest attraction for talents.

Potential versus experience – potential wins

It's basically very simple: stars attract stars. Losers attract losers. And mediocrity attracts mediocrity. That's the way it has always been. It's just that it was never as critically important as today. When the mills of business still ground more slowly and there always seemed to be enough pie to go round, the perceived distance between the leaders and the mediocre players wasn't that great. Today, it is widening dramatically. The winners are expanding their lead more and more. And it's taking less and less time for the mediocre to be threatened with relegation to the loser group.

If you want to prevent that relegation, you have to be fast. There is no time nowadays to hold back until people gain experience. Companies searching for employees who match a certain job exactly because they have years of experience in precisely the right area will become less and less likely to find them. First, because knowledge and experience are becoming obsolete faster and faster. And second, because the best minds will have gone long before such companies get there: gone to where they can develop their talents from day one, instead of having to wait until they are sufficiently "experienced". The decisive factor today is potential, not experience. Why do football clubs have youth teams? Why do classics labels promote youth orchestras? Why do casting agents lurk in front of drama schools? Because they are all looking for talents, and not for "staff".

Fortunately, there are some companies already living this culture. America's Southwest Airlines is one example. It is regularly honoured with the Customer Service Award. When it comes to employees, it "hires for attitude". Yet again, Google is a model here: the company grows and grows and grows. It adds new employees every week. And yet Google does not compromise on the quality of its hires. They have an IQ of over 130 and have survived interviews and tests until they've dropped. And despite this recruitment marathon, Google is considered one of the most attractive employers in the USA. Why? Of course, the relaxed working atmosphere, free canteen and above-average salaries have a part to play. But it isn't just that. Google is an attractive employer not only because it pays well, but because people can work on top-notch projects. And because they have colleagues who are top talents. Talent attracts more talent. And mediocrity … does the same thing.

In theory, many companies are aware of where they should be headed. Unfortunately, practice often limps far behind. People who are quirky and possess inquisitive and critical minds are hard to put up with, and that's a big strain. So when in doubt, many companies still prefer to take well-adjusted "yes" men on board. Personal initiative and decisiveness are about as popular in these organizations as smoking, and a penchant for risk-taking is surgically removed from anyone promoted to middle management – but at least the company pays for the operation.

Boring employees mean boring companies mean boring brands.

Don't get us wrong: it is not about being philanthropic. And it's not about developing young people for altruistic motives. Companies are not charitable institutions. Rather, it's about the market. And it's about profits. The decisive factor is ultimately whether the market will reward what the company does. And in that respect *boring employees* mean *boring companies* mean *boring brands*. Strong brands, on the other hand, are attractive to employees and customers alike, two sides of the same coin.

The German business magazine *Wirtschaftswoche* conducted a survey in 2006 to find out which companies and brands executives considered most fascinating. The result: Porsche, Google, BMW, Ferrari, Microsoft. In that order. Would you care to take a bet on whether more top people apply to any one of these companies than to Hyundai, Lenovo and Nissan combined? Too many people still perceive a brand as the external image of a company and its products. But we have to get our heads round the fact that the brand is concerned with the core, the heart and soul of the company. Managers who have understood that fact and are prepared to embody it will radiate it in every presentation, every public appearance. And if they then ask: "Which of you would be interested in applying for our trainee programme?" – a storm will break loose!

CHAPTER 6

DUMPING BALLAST: FROM TANKER TO SPEEDBOAT FLOTILLA

The old days were better, some people say. Summers used to be summers, winters were winters, the geese were fatter and all the rest. Of course, we would beg to differ. But we don't deny that a lot of things used to be easier. In the good old days, companies just needed one brilliant idea for a phenomenal product, then they could pop the champagne corks and settle down for ten years to come. They had to pull off one major coup and achieve a really strong market position. Then all that remained for the foreseeable future was to water the office rubber plants and manage the accounts.

For example, once upon a time VW launched the Beetle on the market and then confined itself for more than 30 years to letting the funny little car with its characteristic puttering engine roll off the production lines. And making minuscule changes from time to time. The windscreen got bigger here, the windscreen wipers a little longer there. That was the lot. It runs and runs and runs – this legendary German advertising slogan was the management's motto, too. Those were the days!

The salesmen's arrogance was thrown in for free.

Or take Mercedes. In the late 1970s, early 1980s, the company's market position as the producer of the best-quality, highest-prestige automobiles was so strong that the company graciously distributed the cars among customers in the style of an East Bloc Intershop. There was a two-year waiting list for some models – despite their hefty price tag by the standards of the day. The salesmen's arrogance was thrown in for free. The company was basically able to confine itself to three models: small executive class, S-class and SL. An off-road vehicle that was originally developed exclusively for the German army proved too expensive for the men in uniform and was reluctantly added to the product range. And when the compact 190 with its modern styling came on the market in 1982, it was a sensation.

...like sand running through your fingers

The old days were better. Some people say. But times have changed. Gone with the wind. Radically. Forever. Going, going, gone. Unfortunately, a lot of managers still seem to be living in the old days. They are under the delusion that all they need to do is have one stupendously wonderful idea, and they will enjoy a competitive advantage for life.

Anyone who doesn't like globalization should call it up and complain.

But as we have already seen in this book, sustainable competitive advantages that cannot be imitated are snows of yesteryear. We live in the age of globalization. Anyone who doesn't like it should call it and complain. In today's hypercompetitive markets, there are no more sustainable competitive advantages. Richard d'Aveni, professor at Dartmouth College, says: "Chivalry is dead. The new code of conduct is an active strategy of disrupting the status quo to create an unsustainable series of competitive advantages. This is an age [...] of cunning, speed and surprise."

So who will survive in hypercompetition? Not the sluggish supertanker, but a flotilla of agile, manoeuvrable speedboats that can be individually steered by the people in them. Doling out a standard product to the eagerly waiting customer doesn't work any more. Customers nowadays define their demands more and more individually, so that market players have to occupy each new niche as quickly as possible.

Mercedes has got the message. Even experts have to think for a moment when listing the models on the market now: A, B, C, E, G, R, S, CL, CLK, CLS, SL, SLK, ML, GL – have we forgotten one? And the model cycles are getting shorter and shorter. A completely new car is needed in just over six years now, unlike in the 1980s, when it would last for just short of ten.

Zip-zap. Business works MTV style.

Zip-zap. What we are seeing today is a competition of rapidly changing scenes. Business works MTV style. And the good old days are gone forever. It's not going to get any more comfortable, that you can depend on. Why not? What has changed? We live in a world where there are no longer any secrets. No business secrets, at least. Wherever new knowledge arises, it is disseminated immediately, like pollen in spring. And you can be enriched by its fertility or get hay fever. It's up to you.

Wherever new knowledge arises, it is disseminated immediately, like pollen in spring.

At the same time, knowledge can be bought anywhere, anytime. Where Korean automotive engineers used to produce ugly-looking boxes whose very appearance triggered migraine attacks, they are now digging deep into their pockets, poaching BMW's designer-in-chief and attacking the established competition. In this environment, even an innovative flagship company like SAP can nearly miss the boat on Internet technology. Or a company like Motorola can twice come close to going belly-up within just one decade. Companies that keep their majestic ocean liners stubbornly on course are landing in troubled waters at an ever faster rate of knots. Just remember Captain Smith and his unsinkable luxury liner the *Titanic* ...

Backpacks off!

What should you do, then? One thing above all: dump the ballast! It can block a company's access to the nimble lifeboats on every deck. In other words, away with bureaucracy! Stop the megalomania! And once back on dry land, rethink any excess of thoroughness. In what areas has it become an end in itself? And another thing: pull down the Berlin Wall surrounding the company. And do away with conformist structures. If you succeed, you will above all develop a new mindset, in other words, faith in your own strength and the insight gained from personal experience that nothing lasts forever, however impregnable it may appear. And the right mindset is now the most important factor for survival. More important than supposed size and market power.

Files piled as high as the Pyramids of Gizeh.

Let's recap, then: where is the ballast? In four places. Point one: bureaucracy. We were recently invited to a meeting at a large bank in Vienna. No meeting in Vienna is complete without the obligatory strong coffee and glass of water, and this one ran true to form: the banker pressed the well-worn button of his intercom system and called his assistant to place the order. Then he apologized that it would take a while because the bank had now engaged a catering company. A minute later, the door opened and the assistant came in. No, no, she didn't have the drinks with her, but a form which our banker signed off so that the order could be duly forwarded. Ten minutes later the two-man catering team came in with the coffee and water. Of course, they too had a form which had to be completed with details of the reason for the meeting and then signed. All in the cause of good order, and to ensure that this coffee was being drunk purely in an official capacity and not by any chance for personal reasons. And now, the 64-thousand-dollar question: what was getting in the way of innovation at this company?

The 64-thousand-dollar question: what was getting in the way of innovation at this company?

Of course, every manager will say, naturally, I am against bureaucracy. I have been fighting against it for years. There's no such thing as bureaucracy around here nowadays. That may be true if you think of bureaucracy in terms of punching documents and storing them in ring-binders, files piled as high as the Pyramids of Gizeh and mile-long decision paths. But even now that everybody is electronically networked, organized in teams, and can be contacted through short communication paths, has the new *form* of communication really broken down bureaucratic *structures*?

For example, there's the mania that makes a person copy every email he sends to his project manager to 36 other people in the company. The CC syndrome is actually more of a CYA syndrome – short for "cover your ass". Its main accomplishment is to ensure that employees' email in-trays are constantly crammed with messages that are of little or no concern to them, generating a flood of information that makes the ring-binder files of the past look like slender notebooks. But beware of ever deleting anything from your incoming email without reading it. Sooner or later it could be a case of "You were CC'd in on that, why don't you know about it?" And we won't even mention the superstition prevalent at many companies that an email is only a valid document if it is printed.

Superfluous meetings are bureaucracy too.

Or what about the endless meetings of work groups, project teams, committees? We have the impression that in some companies more time is spent per capita in meetings than the people attending them took in aggregate to gain their degrees. The quantity of coffee and snacks consumed in the process would bring tears to the eyes of their family doctors. If the main point of a meeting is to transfer responsibility to a collective, it should be cancelled. Period. Would you care to take a bet that in most companies half of all meetings could vanish entirely from the diaries without anyone missing out on anything?

If the main point of a meeting is to transfer responsibility to a collective, it should be cancelled. Period.

When one of us gave a talk at a German pharmaceuticals group in Amsterdam, something remarkable happened. The company's international management team was invited. The presenter had thought up a nice story – sadly, it didn't work. The story was intended to illustrate the need for experimentation and to show how this actually conflicted with the traditional German spirit of perfectionism.

So he talked for quite a while, and then he asked: "What's typically German?" He was hoping for something along the lines of "German engineering", or even "perfectionism", or at least some harmless cliché like "bratwurst", "Oktoberfest", or "cuckoo clock". Unfortunately, in answer to the question "What's typically German?" the entire room roared as one, "Bureaucracy!"

Kill a stupid rule!

So it's not that people don't realize it. After all, complaining about bureaucracy is an ancient privilege of top managers, in the same sort of spirit as they would say: "Good servants are so hard to find these days." But when will action follow? And what form will it take?

The New Jersey based Commerce Bank runs an initiative called "Kill a stupid rule". Anyone who discovers a superfluous rule receives a $50 reward.

That's much simpler and more effective than a Committee for the Elimination of Bureaucracy that meets for months and in the end only causes more bureaucracy than it eliminates. It is the simple things that actually help us to move forward: show us the three lines in a form that could be omitted, and you have $50 extra for your grocery shopping tonight.

- -

Show us the three lines in a form that could be omitted, and you have $50 extra for your grocery shopping tonight.

- -

The scene shifts to Hewlett-Packard. When the new CEO Mark Hurd took over from Carly Fiorina in 2005, he was completely astounded to find around a dozen management levels between him and his customers. A whole 10,000 out of a total of 17,000 sales employees had administrative jobs – they had no customer contact and never sold anything.

Mark Hurd shook himself up and got going: he merged hierarchical levels and completely reorganized sales. He had realized that nobody today can afford superfluous hierarchical levels and the inevitable bureaucracy that attends them. It's like a competitive swimmer wanting to race in a ballet tutu. The bigger the company, the more its very nature forces it to think about eliminating bureaucracy.

Big. Mega. Megalomania.

Which brings us to point two: megalomania. Any company that wants to solve its problems by constant acquisitions, creating big, fat, inflated structures, will lose out in hypercompetition. Two dinosaurs plan to marry in the hope of becoming one really big, huge dinosaur that may be able to survive the next Ice Age. Think again, pals!

Hans Olaf Henkel, the ex-head of the Confederation of German

Industry, said: "Size is often linked to arrogance and self-satisfaction. Representatives of big business are so courted by the press or their neighbours that they eventually think of themselves as infallible. Which is, of course, nonsense. And if mediocrity is added to that self-satisfaction, they are predestined to go down."

Henkel is right. The pattern is always the same. When a merger is announced, the share price rockets because the company is hopefully going to become so much more efficient. Unfortunately, however, mating and running a race at the same time proves to be a pretty difficult undertaking. Just picture it in your mind's eye. In fact, sober reality presents a different image: there is no evidence that a company will become more profitable just by getting bigger. After the merger, very often widespread disillusionment sets in. Lack of flexibility, internal wrangling and high integration costs destroy virtually every pre-calculated advantage. If the corporate cultures were compatible, at least! But they almost never are. And while the dinosaurs are still working on their merger, the shooting stars have set out to conquer new solar systems.

Mating and running a race at the same time is a difficult undertaking.

So we have to think again. Striving for dominance through mergers can be replaced by temporary internal and external alliances. The more flexible the network is, the fitter it is. At the same time, identity and core values should be strengthened instead of being diluted in a compromise with a merger partner. US company Gore shows how it can be done: none of its units has more than 200 people. That way, it can respond quickly and flexibly to changes in the market. And low-budget airlines Air Berlin and Niki show that there's no need to take out a marriage licence. They cooperate extensively, operate a shared booking website, but remain separate companies.

Thoroughly messed up is still messed up ...

Point one: bureaucracy. Point two: megalomania. Point three: thoroughness. The thing we wanted to get at in the Amsterdam presentation. Don't get us wrong. We don't want to find ourselves claiming on our life insurance after swallowing a headache tablet, or crashing into the nearest field after taking off in the latest Airbus. In other words, in pharmaceuticals or the aircraft industry, extreme attention to detail is undoubtedly appropriate. The question is, however: is it equally feasible in all other industries? We don't think so.

We simply don't have the time any more to test every innovation to death a thousand times over, to examine it endlessly in panel discussions and focus groups, and to iron out every possible residual risk in a subsequent market test. The old sequence of concept development, tests, more tests, and then – but not before that point – a cautious market launch no longer applies. Today, the way to go is to test and adapt, test and adapt. Then test and adapt again. Microsoft and Google simply send their innovations on to the market as beta versions and correct the mistakes during operation on the basis of customer feedback. As long as you remain fair and label beta versions as such, there can be no objection to that. Behind this approach lies a simple truth: companies can only survive if they adapt at least as fast as their operating environment changes.

You may call me Caesar, minion!

One, two, three. Point four: absolutism and Berlin wall building. "I am lord of all I survey. I rule this empire. You may call me Caesar, minion!" Managers who take this as their theme tune will find themselves taking a back seat in the future. In a knowledge society, you will be increasingly unlikely to find all the skills you need within your own company's walls. The example of Procter & Gamble shows how a different approach can work.

In a knowledge society, you will be increasingly unlikely to find all the skills you need within your own company's walls.

CEO Alan Lafley wants to have a rate of 50 per cent (!) of innovations coming from outside the company within the next few years. Lafley's initiative is ruled by the idea that "innovation means networking". Lafley is sending a signal to his product development staff: you don't need to shake the test-tube any more when others have done it already. Instead, look and see how you can network with them. To promote this, Procter & Gamble has created a global network of innovation partners. The aim is to actively draw on external parties such as suppliers, universities, research institutes, or innovation platforms such as NineSigma or Innocentive.

The example of Procter & Gamble illustrates the transformation that innovation management has undergone in many industries over the last few decades: it's time for the classic pipeline model to retire. Innovations arise by a distribution of labour across company borders. There are suppliers of, customers for, and dealers in ideas just as there are suppliers of, customers for and dealers in industrial production. With this move, Lafley is making a radical break with a tradition that has many adherents: mistrust every new idea that comes from outside, because it is new and because it wasn't invented here. That means wall-building. Our contention is, however, that the nature of innovation today is fundamentally different from what is was in the past. Innovation is interdisciplinary. Innovation is global. And innovation is based on networks. Away with the walls surrounding the company! We saw what happened when the East German government cut itself off.

CHAPTER 7

CHANGE OF PERSPECTIVE: FROM "THE PRODUCT IS GOOD" TO "THE FEELING IS GREAT"

Some time ago, we were in London on business. In the evening, we took a stroll through the streets of this fascinating city. At some point, we reached a tube station. We turned round and suddenly found ourselves standing in front of a huge, brightly lit advertising poster. The BMW Z4 Coupe. Wow. The silver-grey sports car was hurtling straight at us. Brilliant design. Amazing perspective. And at the top, in large white letters on a blue background, were just two words: "Radically thrilling".

It struck us both at the same time, that's it, this ad expresses exactly what today's products have to be: radically thrilling. No more talk of acceleration times. No mention of the number of airbags or the anti-corrosion warranty. After all, everyone takes these things for granted in a BMW, because the car is simply state-of-the-art. This is about something completely different: strong emotions, the promise of a unique experience. The visual thrill is converted directly into pure adrenaline.

The visual thrill is converted directly into pure adrenaline.

Radically thrilling! Just a second, isn't that just another verbal ecstasy pill, invented by overpaid advertising nit-wits with gelled-back hair and violet shades? Absolutely not! BMW knows exactly what it's doing in its brand management. The Munich car-maker's strategy can even be described in quite old-fashioned terms: clear values, substance and asceticism. BMW has successfully positioned itself in the market as a premium brand that stands for three core values: dynamism, challenge and culture. These values determine what BMW does in its development departments.

Thrilling to plan – how to create a strong brand

In every step of product development – not just marketing – this automotive engineering company asks the same key questions: is the product truly dynamic? Is it challenging, for example because it embodies strong emotions? And does it fit in with an aspirational, cultured lifestyle? Where does the aesthetic attraction lie that defines the new product as a typical BMW? The decisive factor is that the unique BMW experience is based neither on chance nor on suggestive advertising, but is planned meticulously in every step of the product development process. Every engineer, every technical draughtsman, even every processing clerk knows that he has to contribute his share to this substance. Not once a year at a workshop, but every day. The end product of these combined forces has something solid and meaningful about it. That is not fantasy, it is fact. And rewarded as such by the customer. It's clear enough, of course, that the brand can't go on growing forever. And, in a manner of speaking, it seeks out its customers. In other words, it attracts the people that go with it.

We once discovered the exact opposite at a bank. Fair enough, banks are not exactly famed for having the charisma of the Rolling Stones. But that's totally incomprehensible, when you think about it, because bank transactions are based on nothing else but emotions, with trust first and foremost.

Anyway, some time ago we took part in this financial institution's strategy conference. Once the initial formalities were completed, the CEO introduced us to his colleagues. Man, was he an exciting personality! Not a hair out of place – he could probably control every individual hair by willpower. A three-piece suit, mouse grey. His colleagues, too, adhered exquisitely to the prevailing colour doctrine for their natty suiting: mouse grey, stone grey, pale grey, ash grey. It seemed pretty probable that the suits had been procured by central purchasing in bulk for all the executive staff – we couldn't explain this incredible homogeneity in the dress code any other way.

He could probably control every individual hair by willpower.

The CEO introduced us in a brief speech. He used a draft which had obviously been prepared by his assistant, and which included the following sentences: "They fight with *passion* for the proverbial view over the garden fence, and for liberation from head-to-head competition. They help companies open up market opportunities with – *cool* product ideas." A faint shudder went through him before he uttered the words "passion" and "cool", and he took a long time to pronounce them, as though holding them in the air with insulated tongs.

Of course, he had played right into our hands. With childlike pleasure, we repeated: "Yes, p-a-s-s-i-o-n! Yes, c-o-o-l! Fantastic, exciting, daring. How often do you use terms like that in your day-to-day business?"

They stared at us as though we'd asked why the bankers didn't receive visitors to their branches naked, standing on their heads. Then we explained our point. The more the intangible aspects of their value proposition gained in importance (and what is there about a bank that's tangible, apart from the service foyer and the employees who work there?), the more relevant, useful and important it would be to use words that contained emotions and conveyed a value beyond the pure service.

The idea can also be expressed in less abstract terms: in the detergent ads of the past, when, for example, a resolute lady in pristine white happened to appear beside the washing machine, dealing out sound advice to the mother of some mucky little pups, the aim was to satisfy a certain precisely defined customer need with a product. In a conformist society, these needs repeated themselves millions of times over in exactly the same way. The answer was industrial mass production. Ariel Colour, Ariel Sensitive, Ariel Compact, Ariel Colour&Style, Ariel With Febreze? No way! The superfluity of choice we are faced with today would probably just have confused our resolute white-clad mother's helper.

That was yesterday. Today, in addition to a fantastic and tailor-made product, the customer primarily wants a total experience. And we don't just mean the kind of experience you get in the Disney theme parks or at the cinema. Instead, every company has to think about how we create emotional contacts for the customers. Procter & Gamble has to do it. So does Siemens. So does IBM. And Lufthansa. Or, well, banks. It applies to every company, every department, and every project.

A mug of coffee becomes a happening

Such experiences appeal to several senses, and they have an after-effect, because you can remember them, associated with a positive feeling. They are a happening, something that enriches your life, arouses emotions, and provides something to talk about with friends and colleagues.

For example, the Starbucks experience starts with anticipation. The customer heads into town – and towards a good coffee. Not at some formal, plush tearoom, but at a place where a modern, relaxed atmosphere awaits him. When he chooses his products, he is received by the staff as a friend. The tone is casual. The guest can then settle down and relax with his coffee in a supremely cosy armchair or soft sofa.

And of course, Starbucks also has wireless LAN: in an era where work is a status symbol, no one can afford just to sit aimlessly around in a cafe. Starbucks therefore gives its guests an opportunity to log on to the Internet wirelessly and demonstrate how busy they are, without ever getting up from their seats. The best thing about it is that you can even order your latte macchiato or half double decaffeinated half caff with a twist of lemon online from the barista. This prevents painful errors in syllable stress and intonation and other embarrassing incidents during the ordering process.

The Starbucks experience starts with anticipation.

Starbucks now has fans all over the world. They would never say they had gone for a coffee in town. No, they will say they went to Starbucks. "We have identified a 'third place'," said manager Nancy Orsolini in a television interview. "And I really believe that sets us apart. The third place is one that's not work or home. It's the place our customers come for refuge." In translation: Starbucks doesn't sell coffee, it sells lifestyle.

In our view, precisely this fact explains why the Americans of all people, who historically – to put it politely – were never really conspicuous for their coffee culture, are now plastering the entire world with coffee bars. Despite the fact that the Italians or the Austrians would be a far more natural choice. Only from the point of view of the product, mind you. The Americans have succeeded in making an innocent cup of coffee into a lifestyle sensation. And there's another striking point: the cup of coffee you get at Starbucks is of good quality. If it wasn't, the entire lifestyle thing wouldn't work for long. This way, however, the product is premium, and the prices as well – and the profit margins are correspondingly generous.

Soap dishes, toilet brushes, and juice glasses are not mundane objects, but designer dreams.

Alberto Alessi, whose surname is also the name of a company known to any design fan, once said: "People have an enormous need for art and poetry which industry has not yet understood." Alessi's creed is that soap dishes, toilet brushes, and juice glasses are not mundane objects, but designer dreams. Alessi is not the only company to have realized that. Nokia, Nike and Virgin are all masters of marketing products with a strong lifestyle component. Let's take Apple. The computer brand with the logo that displays an apple with a bite taken out of it has succeeded in making its fans recognize any typical Apple product on sight, despite short product life cycles. Design plays a decisive role. Apple boss Steve Jobs was once asked by a journalist what the special thing about the Apple operating system Mac OS was. His reply: "We made the buttons on the screen look so good you'll want to lick them."

Whatwewantwhatweare

But how many managers really understand what Mr Alessi and Mr Jobs are telling us? Far too few, we would say. Yet we have to emphasize once more that most of them try hard. We were recently invited to give a presentation at a health insurance company. Before our presentation, the managers, filled with pride, showed us the results of the previous workshops. They appeared overwhelming: a new sales offensive, a fresh advertising campaign, new training initiative for sales reps, new furnishings in the branches together with longer opening hours. On top of that, a motivation weekend for staff and a brand new approach to idea management. No question about it, they had been hard at work.

But somehow we felt uneasy in the face of this flood of actions. Certainly, they were all great initiatives in themselves, and we wouldn't have changed a thing. What we felt was lacking, however, was the answer to the most important of all questions: who are you and where are you headed? What makes you u-n-i-q-u-e? What unique experience do you offer your customers? Not just in the branch itself, but on the way there, from the car park, from the bus stop, on the way home? How can you create genuine value for the customers of tomorrow?

Who are you and where are you headed?

Oh dear, that was a sore point. And yet, there are a couple of options available. Health is a meta-trend which is going to become more and more important in the next few years. People used to go to the doctor when they were ill. Today, people would simply like to live healthy lives. But who's going to show them how to do that while so many doctors' offices still see themselves far too much as repair shops? Could a health insurance company find a new role here? Could it be a kind of "health consultant"? If so, the insurer should think about what that would mean to the customer in concrete terms. Where and how can his insurance company help to make him feel strong and healthy?

Emotions everywhere. Yes, everywhere!

In our mind's eye, we can see some people sitting there with arms folded at this point. They're saying that all this stuff about feeling wonderful might be valid enough for service providers. It's easy for international luxury and lifestyle brands to emotionalize their products. And maybe for small niche players, who sell their customers something very special. But I'm in the business to business sector! Or: I'm a network provider. Or: I sell screws. There's no point in all this soft soap about passion and emotion in our industry. That sort of stuff doesn't work for us. Only the facts count.

Our answer is: there is no branch of industry, absolutely *none*, where emotion and lifestyle do not have a part to play. Even in the business to business sector, it's no longer enough these days just to offer a good product. Here, too, customers will opt in the future for the provider that gives them the best feeling, makes them feel understood, suits their world best. Brain research has provided clear scientific evidence that all decisions are significantly influenced by emotions. Our brain works in the same way whether we are on a private shopping spree in a Prada shop or in business negotiations with a supplier for our company.

Wonderful examples of how organizations in the business to business sector can turn their customers into fans through clever brand management and emotionalization have long been available. We particularly like the story of American logistics multinational UPS. Nowadays, no one regards it as a high art to transport packages reliably and fast to any destination in the world, though it is one, of course. However, smooth logistics run noiselessly in the background, and is something that customers simply take for granted. UPS's claim in the USA is therefore: what can BROWN do for you? It's a testimony to a healthy level of self-confidence. You have to be a strong brand for people to immediately associate the colour brown with one of your trucks, in the same way as they associate bright red with mail vans in the UK. But the issue here isn't self-praise. The key words are "do for you".

UPS has taken up the challenge of making corporate man's life easier. The sense of ease and reliability is what UPS is *really* selling these days. If you click on "What can BROWN do for you?" on the UPS website, you will not find a boring product list, but a tool called a "solution finder", where you first have to answer a few questions. For example, what your role in the company is, what industry you operate in, and what your problem is. This way, for example, you can enter that you are a small business person who would like to start trading internationally, but you don't know the game rules. You are then directed to the Global Advisor, part of the website that systematically explains to you what you have to take into consideration in a cross-border exchange of goods. So you don't actually go directly to a UPS product. However, if you've learnt the ropes using the UPS knowledge database, your inclination to entrust UPS with the transport of your first articles to South America will naturally increase. You just sense that your good friend will always be there for you.

Women aiming to sell to other women don't treat them like Barbie dolls.

We have noticed that women have apparently understood this new way of thinking much faster than men. When one of us was at a management meeting of the cosmetics retailer Douglas some time ago, it struck them that of the 140 managers present, a good half were female. We're not concerned here with some kind of quota vehicle, or political correctness. We're talking business, not social justice. Nevertheless, we applaud Douglas. Why? In contrast to the vast majority of its competitors, Douglas has realized that we can no longer afford to do without half of our potential talents.

And another thing: Douglas is a lifestyle company, and the majority of its customers are female. That is the second important insight: women aiming to sell to other women don't treat them like Barbie dolls, but take them and their wants and needs seriously. It's more than that: the company doesn't just want to sell fragrances and makeup, but to fulfil the customers' dreams. A high aspiration? Of course! But a worthwhile one, too.

CHAPTER 8

WE CAN DO IT DIFFERENTLY: FROM OPTIMIZING PROCESSES TO MAKING DREAMS COME TRUE

There is a works council chairman in Germany who drives a Porsche. A silver 911 Carrera S4. The list price is around €90,000. Do his co-workers resent it? No. Is he accused of betraying the working-class cause? No, not that either. And why not? Because he is the works council chairman at Porsche. Let's be honest: there are soft-tops with better fuel efficiency than the Porsche Boxster, and off-road vehicles that have a better drag coefficient than the Porsche Cayenne, and in general there are probably better sports cars than the Porsche 911. Well, we're not entirely sure about that last one. Anyway, there are less costly alternatives. But the Porsche driver buys this car and no other. Why? To live a dream. That's all that counts.

The interesting point is that the employees live this dream as well, even if they don't drive Porsches. They are thrilled to tell every new friend that comes their way that they work for this particular car-maker. And they don't begrudge works council boss Uwe Hueck his 911 Carrera.

It's always the sun. Always. Always. Always the sun!

Deutsche Post/Bahn/Bank also have employees who are proud of their jobs and enthusiastic about the company. We don't deny that. Making a comparison between Porsche and the German banks, railways and postal services, however, is a quick way of clearly showing where the difference lies: Porsche is a merchant of dreams, whereas the others are merchants of products and services. Everyone will agree with us that driving a Porsche or working for Porsche is something special.

What applies to the employees also applies to suppliers, logistics partners, and others: people – men and women alike – are proud to be part of the Porsche legend. And where would any German business or engineering student like to work? Of course, in Stuttgart, for Porsche. And if you can't afford a Porsche yet, you may start by buying a chic pair of Porsche sunglasses to make the waiting easier. As we said above: the sports car-maker is a merchant of dreams.

Where would any German business or engineering student like to work? Of course, in Stuttgart, for Porsche.

So Uwe Hueck, Porsche's works council chairman, can't really drive anything but a Porsche, even though the car has two major disadvantages: a hefty price tag and an even heftier fuel consumption that burns half of Norway's crude oil reserves when you pop out to the baker's in it. But the Porsche driver really doesn't care. In the last few years, this company has managed to emotionalize its products totally. Porsche is about emotion, passion and attachment. And these three principles are at the heart of their business.

What dreams does your company sell?

Most companies haven't exactly been idle in the past few years. However, many of them have spent less time on becoming magnets for customers, employees, and partners, and have attended to the tangible things instead: leaner processes, cost savings, and improving their return on sales. In the course of these endeavours, an unpleasant little accident occurred: customers and employees disappeared temporarily from the management's radar. For example, in the late 1990s, a report was passed down from the executive floor of a Frankfurt bank tower that private customers with assets of less than €100,000 were of no interest because they weren't sufficiently profitable. That hurt. Particularly for the long-standing, less affluent private customers. Employees at these same financial institutions were appreciated just about as much. They were often seen as irritating cost drivers, and in some departments of large banks employees soon came to feel like the "ten little Indians". Let's see who they'll shoot down next. Then there were nine, eight, seven, six ... no wonder *Dilbert* is one of the best-selling business books of all times. In such a situation, humour is a way of suppressing fear, and responding to such circumstances with cynicism is, after all, a way of expressing your rage and disappointment ...

Now, however, most organizations have done their homework. The costs are reduced, the processes lean, the superfluous fat has been cut away ... so what's left to do? Now that companies have extracted the last 10 per cent of efficiency out of the "how?" they have a pressing need to consider the new "what?". After all, process optimization, cost-cutting and efficiency improvement ultimately served primarily to eliminate the mistakes of the past and optimize the status quo.

Recipe for success: shrink to grow?

For years, companies have concentrated on further and further perfecting the Taylorist system. They have vigorously analysed and synchronized workflows. Cost control, quality management and process optimization have been the order of the day. But at some point the whole thing reaches a natural limit. A sprinter can't keep running faster until he only needs one second to reach the finishing line instead of nine point something. It's no longer possible to significantly improve today's world records, however good your high-tech footwear, however tough your performance training, and however perfect your doping.

Today, we see a whole new definition of value creation. From the customers' point of view, value increases the more a product or service enables them to make their dreams come true. A Harley-Davidson insider once described what the motorcycle producer is really offering as follows: "What we sell is the ability for a 43-year-old accountant to dress in black leather, ride through small towns and have people be afraid of him." A Harley is not a means of transport. It is a vehicle for living the dream of freedom and rebellion. It follows that the typical Harley customer is not an ageing revolutionary with a big fuzzy beard, but an affluent gentlemen who longs for freedom and adventure and roars around the countryside on his spine-friendly chopper after a hard week at the office. That Harley is his licence to dream. And that's exactly what distinguishes a strong brand like Harley from weaker brands that only offer solid quality and reasonable prices. Not only the marketing department has to understand that, but every employee.

Today, value added has a whole new definition.

The best companies are now partners in the implementation of life plans. They help people to realize themselves and express their personalities. It's about lifestyle and emotion. But it is about other things as well. After the "lifestyle society", the era of personal transformation is now dawning. As CEO of Ferrari North America, Gian Luigi Longinotti-Buitoni once said something in the same vein as that which we previously suggested about Douglas, the German beauty products retailer. His company was about helping customers to become what they wanted to be. We would add: not just the customers, but all the employees, partners and other stakeholders as well. Magazines like *Cosmopolitan* or *Men's Health* have long earned their money by constantly showing their readers ways to reinvent their looks and shape.

It has always been the offer of a new and better life that has inspired mankind and changed the world. Have you ever been to Belgium or the Netherlands? Every old town in this region, which enjoyed great wealth in mediaeval times, has its "beguinage". The one in Bruges is particularly lovely.

The beguines were a community of Christian women, who had not, however, taken religious vows. They lived together, earned their own money with craftwork, and could leave the community at any time. A priest from Liege created the concept in the year 1180. Today, his idea might be described as a "business model". He grouped neat little houses in a circle on a large meadow before the gates of the city, put a chapel in the middle and invited single women of any age and social standing to live and work there. Some historians call the beguines a "mediaeval women's movement". And the extraordinary thing about this idea was the offer of a completely new life plan. Here, women could lead self-determined lives in a way that could not be found anywhere else during that period. Here, they could make their dreams come true.

Products are emotions. Or not very successful.

And what can we learn from that today? That first of all you have to have a *product*, so that a life plan can become reality. The women's desire for more freedom and self-determination, for an alternative to a life ruled by men only, already existed. But somebody had to come along and build houses on a meadow scattered with fruit trees and offer them to these women so that the wish could become reality. Dreams, needs, wishes – they already exist, and have done from time immemorial. You will be successful if you offer a product that will pick people up from wherever they happen to be at present, and promise them that they can use it to live their dreams, satisfy their needs and fulfil their wishes. Products are emotions. Or not very successful.

Who wants to be a provider of meaning?

Now, there may be managers who feel that "making dreams come true" is laying it on a bit too thick. They do not want to open up new horizons for their customers. They just want to get along somehow. Fine, let them try it. We have no objection. But we didn't write this book for such people.

This book is for the people who are sick of constantly playing it safe. Who do not want to sacrifice their dreams on the altar of conventional wisdom. People who really want to change something. Seeing people stick to the status quo, and being told "we've always done it that way", gets totally on their nerves. They have thought deeply at some point and come up with the conclusion that it's a lot more fun to follow your own North star than to spend all your time pursuing the right thing as defined by other people.

Seeing people stick to the status quo, and being told "we've always done it that way", gets totally on their nerves.

And what would the alternative look like? Does it still exist? In the first part of our book we have talked about how companies walk the well-worn paths of success, and about how difficult it is for them to leave those paths. Most organizations only start looking for new tracks once a life-threatening blockade is already in place on the old one: there's an aggressive swarm of mosquitoes buzzing around ahead, and a herd of elephants approaching at a trumpeting gallop from behind. That's what happened to apparel company C&A.

You would think that the fashion industry would have its finger on the pulse of the times more than any other. But at the apparel company founded by the Brenninkmeyer family in the year 1860 or so, time appeared to have stood still for many years. C&A's massive stores in top inner-city locations offered ladies brightly coloured polyester pullovers, while gentlemen wearing their typical sporty bomber jackets always looked a little bit like security men. The business model worked well, and the many branches of the Brenninkmeyer family got pretty rich on it. Everything in the garden was lovely.

C&A – cool and attractive … isn't it?

The crisis came in the 1980s. C&A were still expanding, but the group was becoming more and more smug. The financial controllers now set the tone. Instead of developing the business model further, those involved wanted to squeeze the last drop out of it. But that no longer worked, because people were becoming more fashion conscious, consuming more and experimenting more. C&A remained cheap and looked it.

At the same time, lifestyle brands aggressively attacked the market, offering young, fresh fashion at the low prices which had once been C&A's exclusive domain. Esprit, S. Oliver and, in particular, H&M won a place in the minds and wallets of teenagers and young adults with their strong brand identities. C&A was out – way out. In Germany, the Brenninkmeyers were left mainly with pensioners, migrants and – East Germans. The pent-up demand from the ex-German Democratic Republic fuelled a last hurrah for the group's financials, but also delayed the effort to solve long-evident problems.

When the crisis could no longer be denied, sales slipped by almost half and the group was deep in the red. Management made frantic efforts to revamp the stores – but with little success. McDonald's at C&A? You could smell the fat used for the French fries all over the stores. Designer clothing? The atmosphere had to be right for people to buy. Hip design for the young and young at heart? Impossible to beat H&M. At the end of the day, C&A just went back to increased attempts to woo its former customer base. No experiments. Good quality, low prices. Hesitantly, customers' interest returned. The economic crisis and a wave of consumer parsimony helped.

But will that be enough for the future? There are a lot of companies like C&A. They stand for okay quality and low prices. But it's not enough, in fact. Danish marketing expert Jesper Kunde sums it up: "You can't survive floating on the tide, assessing the competition, conducting surveys to find out what your customers want right now. What do you want? What do you want to tell the world in future? What does your company have that will enrich the world? You have to believe in that 'it' strongly enough to become unique at what you do."

What do you want? The same as what your customers want? Did Juergen Klinsmann, the former football star and coach of the German national team, ask in the spring of 2006 how he could satisfy the expectations of German football fans? No, he didn't. He did his own thing. And in doing so, he simply broke with tradition. At first, his modern training methods brought him nothing but criticism. Some politicians even wanted to haul Klinsmann up in front of the German parliament's Sports Committee. They wanted to see whether he would satisfy expectations.

Wow, was that a wicked summer!

And afterwards? When the German national team unexpectedly reached the semi-finals of the World Cup, after a string of impressive performances that enthralled the nation, did anyone say "Hmm, the 2006 World Cup satisfied our expectations"? No. We yelled at the top of our voices: "Wow, was that a wicked summer!" We danced in the streets, and the whole of Germany was one big party! Exactly. We lived a dream. Until it happened, we wouldn't even have dared to dream it.

PART 2

FROM EXECUTIVE OFFICE-HOLDERS TO TRUE LEADERS

CHAPTER 9

THERE ARE
NO STAGNATING INDUSTRIES, ONLY
STAGNATING MANAGERS

When preparing for a client meeting a few weeks ago, we got hold of an information brochure produced by an eye-care specialists' association. It was as gloomy as the Vienna Central Cemetery after midnight. The gist was: "The Federal government's socially unfriendly and irresponsible health-care reforms have led to a massive sales slump. Our entire industry feels it has been let down badly, and enormous efforts will be required for a recovery. The number of people employed in our businesses has been falling for years. Fewer and fewer members can afford to train apprentices. In an increasingly difficult environment for our industry, we cannot predict any change for the better in the foreseeable future ..." In other words: victims of circumstance, that's what we are.

Seeing the world through different glasses

We thought for a minute about these poor victims of fate, looked at each other, and had the exact same thought: "glasses: Fielmann". Would the lights soon go out at the expansion-hungry optometrists' chain, too? We did some research, and discovered something astonishing. So far, Fielmann has emerged stronger than ever from every health-care reform programme. That's why the company isn't complaining about the current reforms, which are unlikely to be the last. Fielmann became Germany's leading chain of eye-care specialists in a few short years and has recently enjoyed further expansion. The firm has already provided 15 million German citizens – almost 1 in 5 – with glasses, and now has its sights set on the rest of Europe. Fielmann is one of the biggest training companies in its industry and creates new jobs all the time. In short: Fielmann is a success story that is only just getting into its stride.

Fielmann is a success story that is only just getting into its stride.

How come? The answer is Guenther Fielmann, an entrepreneur who had the courage to challenge the status quo and to part company with all the unwritten rules of the optometry industry. This man did not hesitate to turn those seemingly irrefutable laws of the industry on their heads. Guenther Fielmann is anything but ordinary.

Before the Fielmann era, the unwritten law of the optical industry was to purchase glasses, contact lenses, and cleaning accessories for as little as possible and pass them on to customers for as much as possible. It's clever thinking, of course. Profit margins could be anything up to 300 per cent. In the outlets, stern-featured men in white coats created an atmosphere like that of a doctor's surgery, brooking no contradiction. And if a customer dared to turn up with only the basic prescription from a statutory health insurer and refused to pay an extra charge on top, the profession exacted a bitter revenge. The medical insurance glasses, similar to those provided by the UK National Health Service, transformed cute working-class children into bug-eyed monsters.

Guenther Fielmann sparked off a revolution. His stores offered attractive medical insurance glasses at no extra charge, and thereby removed the stigma of wearing health service glasses. Now, customers could have fashion and chic without paying money on top. But Fielmann also offered branded frames and lenses at lower prices than anyone else. He democratized design, much as IKEA had done in the furniture industry. Soon he was also known as "the Robin Hood of the visually challenged".

Soon he was also known as "the Robin Hood of the visually challenged".

Fielmann became a disruptive force that turned the whole German optometry industry on its head. His strategy was inspired by companies such as IKEA or discount retailer Aldi that showed him how to make a good living even with slim profit margins. The prerequisites were an extensive network of stores, minimal bureaucracy and an ambitious expansion strategy. Guenther Fielmann got to the top in no time. And landed himself in a heap of trouble. The lobbyists of the optometrists' profession spread the word through the media that what he was doing was "unethical". Fielmann was inundated with lawsuits. The company was accused of "price dumping". Finally, however, competitors were forced to realize that Fielmann had simply reduced profit margins to a level that had long been normal in other industries.

But the price was just the start. Through aggressive price competition, Guenther Fielmann won himself scope for action. Now, his aim was not just to be the best low-cost optometrist, but also the most innovative one. The entrepreneur caused a furore when he concluded a special contract in 1981 with Germany's largest statutory health insurance company, the AOK. AOK-insured patients were then offered a choice of 640 fashionable frames "for free", as Fielmann advertised the products he could offer for statutory insurance prescriptions. Then he shocked competitors with his "money back guarantee". Anyone who saw the same pair of glasses at another optometrist's for less money within a certain time would get his money back. His next step was to introduce a three-year guarantee. This was a further snub to an industry where repairs were sometimes almost as expensive as a new purchase. Finally, Fielmann entered into an alliance with insurance companies to offer innovative insurance for glasses. And despite his low-budget philosophy, he was always an excellent salesman. Those customers who genuinely wanted to buy glasses for €10 had to be capable of saying "No, thank you" loudly and clearly to several other offers during the sales process.

How much of Guenther Fielmann is there in you?

Guenther Fielmann's success did not fall into his lap. It took courage, a willingness to take risks, creativity, flexibility, constant learning and personal responsibility. We ask ourselves, and we ask you as well: how much of Guenther Fielmann is there in you? Do we accept the rules of our industries in an attitude of meek humility, or are they a red rag to a bull? Do we really have revolutionary ideas and want to make them reality, or do we prefer to follow everybody else's lead? Do we believe we can change the world, or do we think the system, the law, globalization, or force of circumstance determine our whole lives?

Flowers in the desert – growing against the trend

Do you remember the title of this chapter? No need to turn back the pages, we'll tell you again: there are no stagnating industries, only stagnating managers. Companies that grow against the general trend and are also very successful in stagnating markets come in all shapes and sizes. They can be found in every industry, and they often have to make huge efforts to challenge industry orthodoxies and rules that are as sticky as glue.

Companies like Fielmann did not become successful because they were meticulously following the rules at all times, prudently weighing up any risk, however small, and deciding against action wherever doubt arose. Scaling the peaks demands courage – mostly in the face of prevailing opinion. Criticism is confirmation. Opposition is praise. Hostility is a pat on the back.

In contrast, routine and dogma are the greatest enemies of any entre-preneur or executive. These enemies tempt them into adopting other people's cut-and-dried truths without reflection. Yet when we say that there are no stagnating industries, only stagnating managers, we are immediately peppered with objections from every barrel. You can't really say that, we're told. Instead (please choose any combination of a to c you like), (a) the politicians, (b) the customers, and (c) the competition are to blame for everything.

Anyone can change things, a-n-y-o-n-e!

We are firmly convinced that anyone can change things, a-n-y-o-n-e! Of course, it is marvellously comfortable to make external circumstances responsible for our own misery. For example, how can you make money in retailing if customers are hell-bent on economizing and are hunting only for the cheapest offers? The answer: the same way as fragrance and cos-metics retailer Douglas, for example, where the management has made a clear-cut decision not to follow the low-price trend but to position itself as a lifestyle brand. The result is black figures and steady increases in sales and profits.

Of course there's a correlation between the general economic climate and the willingness of customers to spend money. But even in times of a market slowdown, there are many impressive examples of organizations that survive – and even thrive. The difference between those who see themselves as victims of circumstance and those who do not is their attitude. Moaning is nothing but a diversionary tactic.

Managers cling to excuses so as not to be confronted with the fact that it's up to them to change things. Here are our top ten favourite executive excuses:

1. Globalization is to blame, there's nothing we can do about it.
2. Political conditions have to change first, we need lower ancillary wage costs and fewer laws.
3. We have a consumer downturn at present, people just don't want to spend money.
4. Our industry is cyclical, everybody happens to be in the downswing right now.
5. Our customers don't understand our new strategy yet.
6. You won't find anybody in our industry who does things in a fundamentally different way.
7. In our industry, we have to adhere strictly to EU regulations.
8. Anyone who is still posting growth nowadays is just profiting from the crisis at other people's expense.
9. Times are bad.
10. People are bad.

Okay, that had to be said. Now it's out there. But we still want to go back to looking at how it can be done differently. Because they do exist, the bold entrepreneurs and revolutionary managers. They demonstrate that progress is possible, in good times and in challenging times. These leaders don't just lead a company; they embody it. And what accounts for their success can best be described by the old-fashioned word "virtues". What are the winners' virtues? We are particularly fond of three: channelled anger, healthy megalomania, and willingness to cross boundaries. That needs a bit of explanation, you say? Here you go.

What are the winners' virtues? Channelled anger, healthy megalomania, and willingness to cross boundaries.

The three virtues

First: *anger*. It sounds unusual to start with, even threatening. But we notice it over and over again: true leaders who revolutionize their industries are men and women who are on an "angry mission". They tell themselves: "I can't believe what a mess this industry is in. But I'll give it a go – as long as I get a realistic chance to change something." That's the source from which they draw their energy. And they then direct it into the right channels. Guenther Fielmann was angry about the medical insurance glasses that were as ugly as sin. And the more criticism he attracted, the angrier he got. He once said: "If I hadn't got into so much trouble, I wouldn't be where I am today."

Need any more examples? Here you go: Ryanair boss Michael O'Leary thought the price systems of established airlines were a downright cheek in view of the poor service, and attacked competitors with aggressive advertisements like the German one that said "744 euros: the most expensive cup of coffee". Joachim Hunold, who heads the budget airline Air Berlin, is notorious for his tirades against the trade unions in the editorial of the airline's in-flight magazine. You can argue till you're blue in the face as to whether this is a bright thing to do, but the man is hugely angry – and a successful entrepreneur.

Give Yin and Yang a boot in the behind.

Anita Roddick was once asked what motivated her to found The Body Shop. She replied that it was anger about a cosmetics industry dominated by men who treated women like Barbie dolls, offered environmentally dubious products at excessive prices, and conducted laboratory experiments on animals on top of all that.

Or let's take Goetz Werner, the boss of the dm drugstore chain mentioned earlier in this book. He will not tolerate the fact that there are people in our society who have no access to healthy nutrition or decent personal hygiene. He therefore not only sells organic products and natural cosmetics in his stores at low prices, but is also politically engaged in achieving a minimum wage with no strings attached. He is a man on a mission.

Top athletes have long been aware that an "angry mission" is part of being successful. For them, it's a call to compete, to fight and perform. The important point, however, is to channel the energy produced by the anger into dynamic, responsive and constructive performance. You don't read much about it in management literature. Anger is negative. Anger is aggression. Anger is violence. Anger disturbs harmony. Anger is uncontrolled. Just like passion. Anger is bad, is naughty, is nasty. The preachers of balance say: be at one with the world, in harmony, in the flow, in the swing, think about Yin and Yang … oh, rubbish! Give Yin and Yang a boot in the behind. Anger is pure energy! To really change something in the long term, you have to be immensely angry.

Virtue number two: *megalomania*. No, we're not talking about an obsession with power. We are not advocating megamergers and don't want to justify the "mine, all mine" mentality that some managers have. We're talking about something different, that is, about goals. How big are yours? We say you can't be enough of a megalomaniac. Entrepreneurs and executives who achieve better than average success typically set themselves goals that at first glance look utterly unrealistic. Or even worse: with their objectives set just below the ceiling, they seem totally crazy, mad, ridiculous to outsiders.

Mohammed Yunus, for example, has the big and audacious goal of ending poverty throughout the world. He was ridiculed when he started handing out loans to the poorest of the poor in Bangladesh, even – in a Muslim society! – to impoverished women. To women who were unable to offer any security apart from the promise of paying it all back once they had successfully built up a modest business. Today, the idea that was given life in his Grameen Bank has won Yunus the Nobel Peace Prize.

Dussmann was ridiculed as the "King of the Cleaners".

In the early 1980s, Peter Dussmann recognized the trend towards a service society. When his company Pedus started cleaning hospitals, Dussmann was ridiculed as the "King of the Cleaners", and the "Vacuum Cleaner General". Today, he commands an international service empire worth billions, runs a media department store in a top inner-city location in Berlin, and is one of the most generous patrons of the Deutsche Staatsoper opera company. The man from Swabia, who once trained as a bookseller, now owns castles near Berlin and in Bavaria as well as a villa in Malibu, USA.

It's an oldie but a goodie: no company exceeds its own expectations. If managers think their company can achieve only 1 per cent growth, then it will do exactly that. Max. If managers are of the opinion that their industry is stagnating, they will not move their company forward. Your own convictions and dogma always determine the upper boundary of your capabilities. They are self-fulfilling prophecies. Radical innovators therefore set themselves big, daring goals. That is healthy megalomania.

Which also requires a healthy portion of positive thinking. We don't mean the promises of salvation you get from the you-can-do-anything success coaches, who suggest to their disciples with a mixture of simple messages and New Age esotericism that chickens can become eagles – so long as the borrowed euphoria lasts beyond the end of the motivational seminar. We are talking about a positive basic attitude and ambitious goals. The insight that you will only be successful if you firmly believe you can is attributed to Henry Ford. It also applies in reverse: if you doubt your own prospects of success from the start, you will fail.

Positive thinking does not mean ignoring or refusing to confront setbacks. It's about considering them as temporary occurrences from which important lessons for future success can be learnt.

Finally, the third virtue: *willingness to cross boundaries*. As we have seen, truly successful entrepreneurs and managers do not give two hoots about their industries' limits. Steve Jobs didn't have a Post-it stuck up somewhere that said: "We are a computer company, not a music company." Walter Huber, CEO of the Swiss company Emmi, never said: "We are a dairy company, that's why we don't offer beauty products." Otherwise, he would probably never have succeeded in inventing the beauty drink Lacto Tab with the co-enzyme Q10.

Or there is the story behind a German TV ad from the early 1990s. The screen is dark. A male voice says earnestly and drily with a pronounced Hanseatic accent: "There is no room in Germany for a second news magazine." Then bright colours appear, and a different male voice says: "Oh yes, there is!" *Focus* made its first appearance with this cheeky take on established opinion. Not only did it break the decades-long monopoly of the German news magazine *Der Spiegel*, but it would be impossible to imagine the media landscape of today without it.

The men behind the launch of *Focus* were the congenial twosome Hubert Burda and Helmut Markwort. The publisher and the journalist did not want to accept the dogma that there could only be one news magazine in Germany, with only one political flavour. Others had tried to break *Spiegel*'s monopoly and failed. But, a most unlikely source, the Burda group from Offenburg, more famous back then for its fashion, entertainment and TV magazines, entered the ring to rupture *Spiegel*'s cosy monopoly.

Burda and Markwort didn't need any market research.

Burda and Markwort didn't need any market research. Markwort, an experienced journalist, relied entirely on his gut feel. He dared to do something new, despite working in an industry that has thus far never had a very good reputation for innovation. The courage to "just do it" was subsequently allied with a good dollop of stubbornness. There were dozens of good reasons why *Focus* "had to" fail. Hubert Burda and Helmut Markwort nevertheless carried on with the project and were successful. We need this entrepreneurial spirit more than ever today.

CHAPTER 10

HOMOGENEITY: BENCHMARKING LEADS TO A DOWNWARD SPIRAL

Everybody talks about benchmarking. Managers and consultants are practically obsessed by the word. But we have a problem with this hype. Sure, the underlying idea makes perfect sense: it is about learning from the best. It's just that in the vast majority of cases people compare themselves with the best from their own industry.

If you are constantly comparing yourself with others, you will become mainly more comparable.

And that's what troubles us: if you are constantly comparing your company with others from the same industry, or your division with other departments in the same company, you will become mainly more comparable.

But if you want to change things for the better, adapting to others is poor advice. If personal success is your goal, it is not enough to get up at six o'clock, eat muesli and scratch your right ear three times. And if you want to create new value, so that your company will still be profitable tomorrow, benchmarking won't help you.

Benchmarking and best practices should be struck out of our vocabulary. These words are nothing but synonyms for "copy & paste". Everyone copies each other in the hope of making progress. In actual fact, that only helps the absolutely god-awful to rise to the heights of mediocrity. You can't copy your way to the top, though. You have to change the rules of the game. And that is only possible by seeking benchmarks outside your own industry.

If you want to change things for the better, adapting to others is poor advice.

We travel a lot, and often stay in hotels. We are repeatedly astonished by how much one business hotel seems to be an exact replica of the next. You can wake up anywhere in the world and ask yourself in some confusion: "Where on earth am I today?" It isn't necessarily because of the amount of red wine you drank the night before. It's more because not only the rooms, but other hotel services as well, seem to have been getting more and more alike over a period of years under some mysterious cross-company, cross-border standardization programme. That's why hotel guides have developed little pictograms offering a comprehensive description of every accommodation. Hotel A and Hotel B are in the same category if they offer exactly comparable services.

It can be done differently, as we found out some time ago in the Four Points Sheraton at Los Angeles Airport. This hotel has realized that they won't impress the market by hyping up the same run-of-the-mill stuff you'll find in any other business hotel in the world. We've mentioned checkout before: at the Sheraton the room is rented for 24 hours, regardless of when you check in. Yippee! And alongside other innovations, the hotel has a "gourmet takeout before takeoff". Yippee again! Because if you've been on many American domestic flights, you'll know that the inboard food frequently veers between insult and assault. The problem opens up a brilliant gap in the market for the Four Points Sheraton. Really delicious snacks such as Grilled Chicken Breast Sandwich, Fresh Fruit Medley or Shrimp Louis Salad can be ordered from room service shortly before departure. And later, on board the plane, the flight attendant can be sent on to the next seat with a friendly, smiling "No thank you". Why have so few other hotels discovered this?

Painting by numbers, or Picasso?

Of course, one or two such ideas won't make a hotel chain's sales explode. But a whole bunch of them might. A continuous ideas pipeline has to be installed, and old habits should be challenged over and over again. Here, too, the mindset makes the difference. What would you prefer to be: model pupil or innovator? If you want to be a model pupil, by all means go on trying the painting by numbers method. Pursue external benchmarking in your industry and keep copying from other people's latest templates.

But – Picasso never copied Matisse. With the exception of Konrad Kujau, the swindler who sold 60 volumes of forged "Hitler Diaries" to a German magazine, few copyists have ever become famous. Only techno-crats, bean-counters and cravens say: "Let's do exactly the same as every-one else." A real leadership personality seeks his own path. And he follows it even when he can clearly see that it will be the stonier one.

Picasso never copied Matisse.

We are convinced that executives need to think beyond the familiar and to challenge conventional wisdom. That isn't always easy – not so much because the managers don't see the need to get new, innovative ideas into their heads but more because of the difficulty of getting rid of the old ones. They are so used to what is going on in their industry that they stopped questioning it. You can only get rid of that particular type of blindness by turning around and looking beyond the borders of your industry.

Some years ago, one of us was involved in a large research project which required them to visit some major banks. Lying in bed at night, they hon-estly couldn't remember which banks they had been at during the course of the day. If fifty top managers from each of these banks had been swapped for competitors' executives at random in the night when everyone was asleep, it's doubtful anyone would have noticed the difference in the morning. Because the strategy would not have changed one iota.

The one tragic thing about it was that each of these financial institutions was absolutely convinced that it was quite different from the rest. When the similarity was mentioned to them, the reaction was always outrage: "No, honestly, what can you be thinking of? You really can't compare us with one of the others. We are absolutely different in every respect." And the ques-tion of whether the customers would agree was answered in tones of deepest conviction: "Of course our customers would n-e-v-e-r confuse us with them." Their scandalized faces stated quite clearly: "Only a complete imbe-cile with no idea of our industry could ever assume that we were pretty much the same!"

Wheat and chaff, or how to spot a successful manager

To get to the bottom of this gap between people's self-perception and the way in which they are seen by outsiders, we ask a few questions in our workshops:

Question 1: Do your competitors consider you more of a rule-follower or rule-breaker?

Question 2: Has your strategy changed significantly in the last few years? Have you acquired a new customer segment, conquered a new market, built new skills? Has the structure of your revenues and profits changed as a result – or has everything somehow or other stayed the same?

Question 3: Has it become harder for you to attract top talents? Do they want to work for you, or do they howl with laughter when you offer them a job?

The answer to this last question is a simple but always wonderfully accurate indicator. The ability to attract the best minds to your company shows very clearly how you are regarded by outsiders.

Do the best people want to work for you, or do they howl with laughter when you offer them a job?

Often, the sobering realization after this first round of questions is: "We do business as usual." Please don't get us wrong. We neither tell people what they should have done nor blame them for what they do. On the contrary: those who manage to admit to themselves that they have always just done everything the same way as everybody else are already halfway to leaving the beaten track. The stupid thing is that our mindsets gear themselves to what is perceived as normal and successful in our own industries. That very process has been thoroughly dinned into most of us in the course of our careers. But there are ways to break out. To take them, managers first have to realize clearly where they and their company actually stand. So we ask them which of the company's values are rewarded by the customer. Typically, this sparks off an argument in the group, because everyone thinks his own department is the biggest value driver.

By way of illustration, we next draw a matrix of the individual value drivers. Let's assume we're talking about an airline. The value drivers from the customer's point of view could then be, for example: safety, staff friendliness, number of destinations, quality of inboard food, punctuality and so on. Then we ask the workshop participants to estimate how much the company differs from the industry average on each of these value drivers. When we have gone through all the points, the result is virtually always the same. The curve shows practically no outliers. It is the value curve of the entire industry, the perfect benchmark.

Sometimes, a few people will then say spontaneously: "So we presumably have to get better on every point." And we say: "No, you don't. There are three options: either become *radically different* and therefore *extremely superior* in one driver. Or completely *eliminate* one driver, or reduce its value to a minimum, because it makes no difference from the customer's point of view. Or, the third possibility, *add* a completely new value."

For example, an airline could differentiate itself radically from others by doing away with the extreme inflexibility of flight tickets. Lufthansa, for example, currently charges astronomical prices for a fully flexible ticket, and business travellers grit their teeth and pay. It would be great to see an airline with the kind of pricing that enables it to say: a ticket from Frankfurt to London is available at a reasonable price – and the reservation can be changed at any time. Suddenly, freedom would be restored to travel.

Less means more value in this case.

Ryanair demonstrates why it can make sense to eliminate a value. It doesn't do food on board. As a result, customers pay less for their tickets. And Ryanair's target group rewards precisely that. Less means more value in this case. Of course, it is particularly aspirational to identify and add on totally new value drivers. You do need a bit of imagination there, though. Virgin Atlantic had a particularly clever idea for its flights from London to the USA. Business Class passengers are picked up from the city centre by motorbike. A little uncomfortable? Perhaps. But they race past every traffic jam and get to Heathrow faster than ever before.

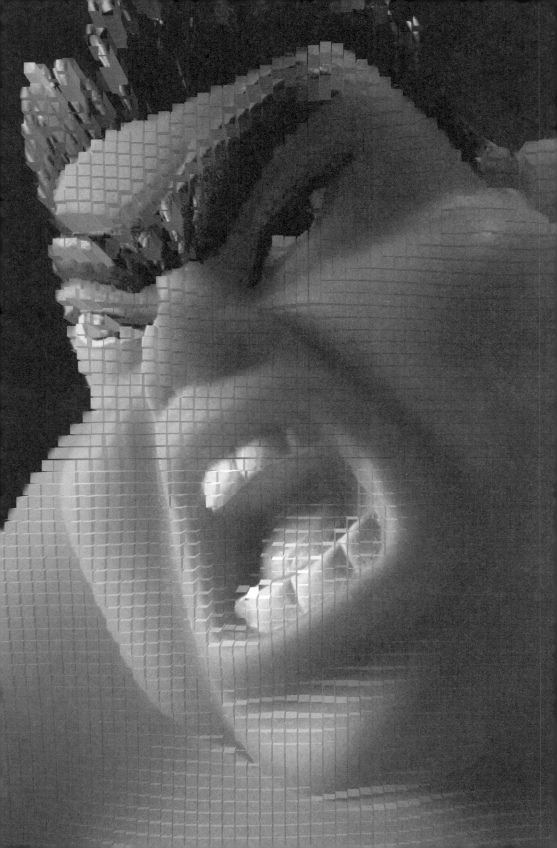

CHAPTER 11

UNSEXY: MANAGEMENT TOOLS ARE ALWAYS PASSÉ

Our book *Marketing Trends* has been on the market for a few years now. The book is based on a study of 550 managers who were interviewed about the most important marketing tools. We summarized the data, distilled trends and poured them into the book, garnished with hints and tips. From the time of first publication, the underlying study has been available on our website and can be downloaded free of charge. What can we say? After all these years, the study is still downloading like hot cakes.

We know what makes the study so compelling: everyone wants to know what the hottest trend is. Everyone wants to possess the wonder drug of marketing, the magic tool that eases every stubborn nut and bolt in the customer relationship. And if the majority of respondents says that customer relationship management is the most important tool, then everybody, literally everybody, naturally wants to do CRM. And of course, no one can afford to ignore the things that have been ranked second and third. After that, however, attention spans are exhausted. If lifestyle marketing is only in seventh place, basically no one cares any more.

For every problem there is a solution in 3.5 simple steps. – Hmmph. There should be. – There may be. – It would be nice if there were. – Maybe it really exists? Pity it doesn't exist. – Fine, it doesn't exist. Nevertheless, we are all looking for something that gives us direction and inspiration, something that gives us answers, something easy to digest, something simple, practical, that you can present with effortless ease.

The Druid's magic potion that will make my sad old shack into an invincible fortress.

Solutions in 3.5 simple steps are a growth market. It's not only American televangelists who thrill the masses with promises of salvation. Self-appointed business experts do the same thing. Typically, it goes like this: a manager, racked by self-doubt, picks up a business magazine or universally praised management bestseller and reads about some revolutionary programme with an electrifying name like "Re-engineering-Six-Sigma-Total-Quality-Tarzan-management". Even after the first lines of the description the manager feels a tingling sensation in his brain. Could this be it at long last, the long-awaited Druid's magic potion that will make my sad old shack into an invincible fortress? Sounds fantastic … let's see if I can make it work for me …

As soon as he's back in the office, an appointment is arranged with a management consultancy that will be happy to help the company implement the new tool. The consultants present an awestruck audience with columns of figures and brightly coloured charts and intone optimism-laden words till their cufflinks crack and the soft drinks in their glasses start to simmer. They can barely contain their enthusiasm: "Re-engineering-Six-Sigma-Total-Quality-Tarzan-management will, nay, *must* be the solution to all the problems of the Western world." There's no time to lose. Project teams are called frantically into life, reports written, and the diary crammed with meetings. After a while, however, it becomes evident that the desired turnaround is obstinately refusing to materialize. At this point, the next project phase is reached: the guilty party has to be found. That doesn't take long. It's all this American rubbish that was dumped on the company by those consultants. They're all blood-suckers, they just pocket outrageous per diems and do nothing. That's the management's conclusion, which we've censored to protect the young and innocent. The Managing Board declares the project a failure, and the company gets back to business as usual. Until the next industry conference where a euphoric speaker proclaims a radical new solution to every business problem … (fade out).

But who is really to blame? The consultants? The management gurus? The American Dream? Christopher Columbus? Let's rephrase the question: who buys in the consultants? Who wants to have the tools? Who creates the enormous demand for ever more new wonder drugs for management use? Well?

You can do yourself a nasty injury with traditional tools as well.

And it's by no means just the short-lived management methods with the mellifluous, mysterious names that you need to be wary of. You can do yourself a nasty injury with traditional tools as well. Tools, methods, instruments – they are all there to help you think, no more and no less than that. They cannot replace your own creativity and activity. They are useful provided you use them in moderation, always think for yourself as well, take the necessary responsibility, acknowledge your mistakes and learn from them.

You need to look through the windscreen!

The classic management tools in particular induce executives to put their brains on standby. An example? The dictatorship of market research. Basing strategic decisions and product innovations on market research is like driving using only the rear-view mirror. Not just for parking, at that, but in fifth gear on the motorway. Market research is always a car's length behind, because it determines the results of yesterday's decisions. In doing so, however, it also whispers in your ear that yesterday's solutions can solve tomorrow's problems – but they can't.

Market research is always a car's length behind.

Speaking of motorways ... Do you sometimes listen to the car radio, on longish trips, for example? The nice thing about it is that you don't actually have to search for your favourite station. Just switch on. It really doesn't matter which station you're listening to, the sound is the same everywhere. An entirely uniform wall of noise. "The greatest hits of the 1980s, 1990s, and the best music of today" is the proud boast of DJs everywhere. Ten hours on the A7 motorway that runs from the Danish to the Austrian border, and the only thing that changes is the lettering on the radio display. The backdrop of the last 30 years' mainstream pop remains the same. The mixture is enriched with a bit of news, information, weather and traffic reports. And the final touch is the violation to your ears from the advertising spots, because after all, the station needs something to live on.

There's no question: competition between radio stations is fierce. Which makes it all the more perverse that nearly all of them are convinced they can win it with more and more of the same. At one workshop we ran for a radio station, the management's guiding force emerged quite clearly:

market research, market research and more market research. It determines every single element of the programme. Stations want to be absolutely certain of not having the wrong programming, so listeners are constantly surveyed about their preferences. Managers measure audience figures with the meticulousness of professional seismologists. Panic breaks out at a feather's touch downwards, and they frantically start to revamp their programme design.

In this kind of corporate culture, asking employees to be innovative is about as effective as prohibiting people from picking their noses at red traffic lights. Management focuses its tunnel vision on the current results of market research, and any trace of creativity and innovation is killed right away. And yet, the question of what listeners want is not the key to truly unique programming. Don't get us wrong. Of course you should listen to your customers. But that doesn't mean you have to reproduce everything the customer says in faithful detail. Because what the customer is telling you is yesterday's news, not today's.

Asking employees to be innovative is about as effective as prohibiting people from picking their noses at red traffic lights.

The ideas and concepts we need from management are the ones that today's customer hasn't yet thought of, the ones he can't want today because he has never heard of them. British architect Sir Denys Lasdun once said: "Our job is to give the client … not what he wants, but what he never dreamed he wanted; and when he gets it, he recognizes it as something he wanted all the time."

We tried to make clear to the managers at our workshop that precisely this obsession with what the listener wants had become the industry's biggest problem. As long as you stick slavishly to the dictates of market research and make every corporate decision dependent on its direct influence on ratings, you shouldn't be surprised that you have no unique selling proposition. It's a vicious circle: the station plays what the audience "wants" and the audience "wants" what it's used to. The problem with that is that what we are used to is also what we take for granted, and there comes a point when it no longer attracts any particular attention.

Tim Renner has proved with Motor FM that you can be very successful on the private radio market even if you cut yourself free from the dictates of market research. The station, which you can tune into in Berlin and the Stuttgart area on terrestrial radio and otherwise on the Internet or by cable, really is anything but ordinary in comparison with its competitors. The difference starts with the choice of music, which creates an entirely individual sound that can most readily be pigeonholed as alternative – heavy on the guitar and with some raw edges to it. The music is the clear identifying anchor for listeners.

Yet Motor FM does not constantly ask its listeners for their favourite songs; it offers them what the editorial team likes. It doesn't always have to come from bands with established cult status; it could be a new band from Berlin's trendy district of Friedrichshain. However, the station does not just differentiate itself from competitors by its music, but also, and particularly, by its business model. After all, constant promotions of furniture stores or the latest absorbent kitchen paper would be most unlikely to fit in with their selection of music. So Motor FM has tapped into other sources of cash.

The station has gone for live events, Internet downloads that they charge for and cooperative deals with industry and retailers. For example, the station has its own special shelf in the Berlin media department store Dussmann, one of the capital's biggest CD retailers, where customers can find the music the broadcaster is featuring at any given time. Yet if Tim Renner had conducted market research, he would probably have reached the conclusion that people wanted to listen to "the greatest hits of the 1980s, 1990s, and the best music of today".

It's better to know the customer than the studies about the customer

What is market research actually good for, then? You don't need to throw the baby out with the bathwater. Just don't expect too much from it. It is what it is: a look in the rear-view mirror. If you keep your eyes to the front and look through the windscreen most of the time, it does make absolute sense to cast a glance backwards from time to time as well. For example, when you are observing customers' reactions to innovations and want to draw lessons from them for future innovations, or if you want to adjust your strategic direction and your product range. But the important thing is to make sure that analysis does not become a substitute for action.

And another thing: field research is better than market research. If you know your territory, you don't need a surveyor. If all the employees in the company simply listen to customers and are in constant dialogue with them, that's worth more than any market research. You get a lot less out of asking a customer "Would you buy that?" than from simply spending time getting to know him, whether in project teams or on local visits to wherever your target group may be. Field research also means developing your own methods of being closer to the customer.

Ex-Aldi manager Dieter Brandes tells how Aldi decided on its product range when the German retail giant entered the Turkish market. The local managers simply asked as many families as possible to keep the receipts from their weekly shopping. The product assortment was then put together according to the information obtained, and was an immediate success. That wasn't innovative as such, but at least it was clever. Companies that view themselves as highly innovative, such as the Californian design and innovation consultancy IDEO, typically do not do any market research at all. "Customers in most cases won't be able to tell you what you need to know," IDEO boss David Kelley once said.

The customer may simply not have the vocabulary to be able to articulate what isn't right with the product range, and in particular may lack a sense of what's missing. That's why, if you want to improve a product or develop a radically new market offering, it's essential to observe people with your own eyes, as an "anthropologist" so to speak. By doing that you are trying to find out what potential buyers actually need. Innovation psychologist Leon Segal says: "innovation starts with an eye".

When you emancipate yourself from market research, you've taken the first step towards liberating yourself from trusting in all those other management tools that – only apparently – indemnify executives from personal responsibility. Rid yourself of the notion that you can install an autopilot in the management cockpit. That autopilot will never be invented. Never.

Even the term strategic planning is self-contradictory.

We are writing about innovation and about how you can outmanoeuvre the competition with fresh and clever ideas. But the big question is: where are these fresh and clever ideas supposed to come from? Are they generated during the annual planning process at your company? Yes, maybe? Possibly? Well, strategic planning, like market research, is a very popular management tool. But we maintain that *you cannot create innovation with central planning*. Period. If central planning with all its "instruments" had ever created anything innovative, then Silicon Valley would be closer to Moscow than San Francisco.

Even the term strategic planning is self-contradictory, because it assumes that an economy is a plannable parameter managed by executives.

Classic strategic planning assumes that market developments can be predicted with the aid of existing heuristics, algorithms and assumptions. But the business world is largely unpredictable. Leaving the responsibility for "planning" the future to strategic planners is like asking a bricklayer in front of a heap of bricks to create Michelangelo's *David* with his trowel in one hand and his bucket of mortar in the other. Strategic planning is not a suitable tool for dealing with the future.

And tomorrow? Haven't a clue. But totally different, anyway!

The reason is simple: every planning process builds on certain prerequisites – technologies, capital market, customers, cash flow, innovation, market value, sales revenues, geopolitics etc. Today, all these parameters are just where they happen to be. And tomorrow? Haven't a clue. But totally different, anyway! The prerequisite for a flourishing business today could be completely irrelevant tomorrow.

That doesn't mean that you shouldn't do any planning at all, and cheerfully pursue your business on a day-by-day basis. Go ahead and plan! The point is that strategic planning lulls you into a false sense of security. Planners assume that around the same number of people who decided to buy your product last year will also buy it this year and next year – plus or minus a few per cent, perhaps. So people think that a process labelled "last year" will simply repeat itself. No one can afford to be that naive.

CHAPTER 12

COURAGE: MANAGERS WHO MAKE MISTAKES (AND ALLOW THEIR EMPLOYEES THE SAME PRIVILEGE) ARE MORE SUCCESSFUL

In the late summer of 2006, the German business magazine *Wirtschafts-woche* did some research into the subject of error friendly culture. The article was supposed to be about the way failures were dealt with and managers' readiness to learn from them. To that end, the magazine would have liked to present top managers' stories along the lines of "My biggest mistake and what I learnt from it". However, the inevitable happened: not a single executive was willing to admit in public that he had ever charged off bald-headed in the wrong direction.

Instead, managers tried to peddle their latest great deeds to *Wirtschaftswoche* as supposed errors, the cases that had been transformed into gushing wellsprings of cash under their own magical hands. The prize-winning effort was by the owner of a sausage factory who praised his latest innovation, chest swelling with pride: a pâté sold in a plastic cup instead of in natural intestine. What does that have to do with an error management culture? Well, he felt he had made a mistake in not having had this sensational idea sooner! The business weekly ultimately published an article on error friendly culture that was larded with managers' success stories. How bizarre!

Errors? Away with them!

This story reminds us fatally of job interviews we had when starting out in our careers. To be honest, we look back on these interviews with extremely mixed feelings. We were always asked the same question over and over again: "What do you see as your biggest weakness?" Or: "Have you ever made a real mistake?" It's obvious that every human being has weaknesses and makes mistakes from time to time. Anyone who seriously denies that this applies to him personally is ready for the padded cell!

Never answer these questions honestly, even if held at gunpoint.

But of course, we all know the unwritten rule of job interviews, which goes as follows: never answer these questions h-o-n-e-s-t-l-y under any circumstances, even if held at gunpoint. For example, if you respond with "Sometimes I can't concentrate for a whole morning at a time" or "I once threw away thousands on a completely idiotic idea" you may as well go straight home, having achieved nothing more than waste four hours with screaming kids on an overcrowded train. You will have failed even if you regularly have Nobel Prize-worthy ideas in the afternoon and have already earned millions for your previous employer, in addition to having the faults you have honestly set to your own account.

What the job interviewer actually wants to hear are supposed weaknesses that are really strengths. "Mistakes" that turn out to be heroic deeds when considered in the full light of day. Something like: "My work fascinates me so much that I often can't stop in the evenings and stay in the office until three o'clock in the morning." This is pretty sick behaviour for a poorly paid person in dependent employment. But it is very popular with potential bosses. It is also particularly clever to accuse yourself of "impatience". The idea here is: I'm so dynamic, I just can't sit still. In the days when German daily newspaper the *FAZ* ran its regular Friday column in which it asked prominent people to complete a questionnaire, nine out of ten managers and politicians replied to the question about their biggest fault with: impatience. How could they undertake this self-flagellation with such unflinching boldness! You have to respect them for it.

Typically, it is the highly creative minds who think differently. Members of the new Creative Class. They are characterized by a highly pragmatic attitude to failure. They say things like "I was knocked back once, but I learned from my mistakes, and now I'm back in the race." And what if they fall flat on their faces again? Doesn't matter – somehow or other life still goes on. Lessons learned. And yes, they would take the same risk again, any time.

Take venture capitalists in Silicon Valley, for example. Their portfolios are broadly designed in accordance with the expectation that setbacks and even total flops will happen. One venture capitalist told us that if just one investment in ten was a hit that would be absolutely wonderful. You simply have to accept the other nine, because nobody can suspend the laws of probability. On the other hand, a big hit can become a global success at lightning speed, and more than make up for the failures.

That's refreshing. Yet in too many organizations, managers' conceited behaviour in depicting themselves as fault free is considered good form. That's pretty neurotic. Even worse: making mistakes is considered equivalent to failure. In this kind of culture, risk-taking propensities are surgically removed from anyone promoted to middle management – but at least the company pays for it.

Inactivity is the worst mistake – and the only one that should be punished.

This kind of basic attitude leads to inactivity and ultimately to paralysis. First the employees are paralyzed, then the department, then the firm, then the country's entire economy.

But in a company that aims to be innovative, inactivity is the worst mistake – and the only one that should be punished. Inactivity is like a creeping disease where the people who are rewarded are the ones who are so risk-averse that they sit on their behinds and don't move, and therefore *cannot* make any mistakes. What's needed is intelligent handling of errors, through which people learn to profit from them.

Towards a golden future, false step by false step

In one of his books, Tom Peters tells an illuminating anecdote about the founder of American retail giant Wal-Mart, Sam Walton. Every time Walton had an idea that absolutely did not work, he would arrive at the office the next morning giggling like a schoolboy and say something like: "Well, at least that's one dumb idea out of the way. Now, where were we?" And yet Walton detested sloppiness and laziness like poison. He simply lived by the motto of testing every idea vigorously straight away. And if it went wrong, he would test the next one with even more vigour.

It is well known that Wal-Mart has recently been an enormous flop in Germany. And that's precisely why we are telling you this story. If the same thing had happened to Lidl or Metro in the USA, it would undoubtedly have shaken these companies to the core. Heads would have rolled, strategies would have been challenged and the PR department would have had to denounce the culprits publicly on behalf of the top managers: incompetent politicians, unfair competitors, insecure consumers. In such a situation, Wal-Mart says: "Now, where were we?" Who dares loses now and then. The next bold endeavour can be another major hit.

But in many organizations, top management would rather crawl naked over broken glass than risk anything really new. This leads to a tremendous play-it-safe mentality that paralyzes any desire to innovate. And yet people know they're not infallible. In theory, most of them even realize they've got to be bolder and more willing to experiment, not to be even more perfect. Nevertheless, they waste most of their energy on trying to make out that every decision is the act of a group wherever possible. If anything goes wrong, nobody's to blame. Hegel and Marx are surprisingly alive and well on many executive floors; if the place is slowly but surely going down the tubes, the *Weltgeist* or history is guaranteed to be the culprit. Not a human being, at any rate. But if something turns out well, the manager will prefer to go with Nietzsche and declare himself a superman. Until the next risk crops up and has to be meticulously ring-fenced.

In many organizations, top management would rather crawl naked over broken glass than risk anything really new.

The alternative is: courage. To be an innovator and to dare to do something new means departing for unknown shores. NB: with no guarantee of success. Naturally, only executives who believe in themselves, who have courage, confidence and faith in their own strengths, can do that. And that also includes instilling a culture where employees do not constantly fear failure, but are allowed to experiment as well. Concealing mistakes is a sign of fear and weakness. Australian executive Phil Daniels once said: "Reward excellent failures. Punish mediocre successes."

The next virtue is: trust. That means building on your ideas and your team and trying things out even when all the self-appointed experts prophesy that the experiment will fail. Trust doesn't mean obstinacy at all costs. But it does mean a healthy adherence to your own convictions. To convictions that could land you flat on your face at times. But herein lies the strength of the leader: resilience. Getting up again very quickly after defeats and going on – over and over again. Ultimately, mistakes are nothing but a necessary, integral component of all progress, all innovations, all new forms of value creation. You can only reduce your innovation error rate to zero by preventing all innovation. Thomas Watson, the founder and former CEO of IBM, once said: "If you want to succeed, double your failure rate."

That's exactly the point. Empirical research has shown that creativity results from high productivity more than anything else. This law is confirmed wherever you go, whether we're talking about managers, inventors, scientists, poets or painters. Thomas Edison, Leonardo da Vinci, Albert Einstein or Pablo Picasso. They were all geniuses in their own fields. But they're linked by something else as well: they were very much more productive than their contemporaries. Part of their success stemmed from the fact that they dramatically increased their failure rates. For example, Einstein conducted a verbal duel with the Danish physicist Niels Bohr for many years. Einstein was determined to refute quantum mechanics. Ultimately, he failed in his attempt because he hadn't taken his own theory of relativity into account. It may have been this misfortune that led Einstein to the conclusion: "The only sure way to avoid making mistakes is to have no new ideas."

If you want to succeed, double your failure rate.

In theory, many people will agree with that. However, managers also have to live this insight and embody it externally. They have to consciously walk the talk. Even if you have 98 per cent of the information you need for a decision, it is often the remaining 2 per cent that decides whether you generate a profit or a loss.

We have to experiment in order to get on the trail of innovative and inspiring solutions. And we have to learn to see mistakes and wrong decisions as triggers for our next experiment. We just have to "think of something". Of course there's no guarantee that the experiments will deliver the hoped-for success at the first attempt. Or at the second attempt. There is no such thing as guaranteed success.

That's why you need many stupid, bad and off-the-wall ideas to produce one good one. No one knows in advance exactly which one will be a waste of time and which one will produce the next iPod. Thomas Edison, perhaps the greatest inventor of all time, made more than 9000 experiments before he came upon the light bulb. Does that make the first 8999 failures? No. They were the road to success. To be successful, you just have to make enough mistakes.

Always shoot for goal!

Management used to be like golf: calmly get set for each stroke, concentrate, hold your posture. And above all: always keep your handicap low! Today, management is like football. Shoot for goal whenever the opportunity arises. A single goal in the 89th minute can be enough for you to win the game. But to get it, you have to try often enough. The striker's motto is: go for it!

Richard Branson is that kind of striker in the management field. Over the past years and decades, his Virgin group, which started as a small mail order record business in London in the year 1972, has developed into a real multi-brand – you could even call it the first multinational street kiosk in the world. In addition to the core start-up businesses of music (Virgin Records, Virgin Megastores) then airlines (Virgin Atlantic, Virgin Express), the group is now represented in more than 50 other product categories.

The most important connector between the far-flung provinces of the Virgin empire is Richard Branson himself. Like a kind of modern Robin Hood, he has been breaking the rules of his target markets for years, but always delivers high quality and, with British humour, satisfies his customers' need to rebel against the establishment with Virgin products. Branson's explanation of his approach is that Virgin goes for industries where customers are just being ripped off, identifies how they could be given a better deal, and improves the brand in the process.

In doing so, the British multimillionaire is pretty well aware that only some of these activities will be worthwhile in the longer run. However, he always manages to kick the ball back to the goalkeeper in time. In other words: an essential part of every new business plan is an effective exit strategy. Over the course of the years, Virgin has dropped a lot more things than other companies with a hundred years of tradition behind them have ever tried out. He is not in the least worried by flops like Virgin Cola or Virgin PCs. Next up, he wants to make space tourism affordable and build a hotel in space. He has the moon in his sights.

"You miss 100 per cent of the shots you don't take" could be Branson's creed. But the person who actually said it was Canadian patron saint Wayne Gretzky, whom many people consider to be the best ice hockey player of all time. Who would care to contradict him?

But careful! Not all mistakes are cool. On the contrary, there are errors of workmanship that are simply inexcusable. These have to be clearly distinguished from the courage to venture something new. We recently gave a presentation at a newly opened hotel whose English owner wanted to make it the best home from home in the German capital.

But careful! Not all mistakes are cool.

We think it's a brave move not to try to outdo competitors in the five-star-plus segment with even bigger crystal chandeliers and even more silver on the tables. This hotelier has moved into a bank building constructed in 1889 in Italian Renaissance style, and the layout has simply been accepted, though it is, shall we say, less than perfect for a modern hotel.

So far, so good. But shortly before the start of the event, total chaos broke loose in the hotel. First there was no microphone, then no loud-speakers. Improvisation solved these problems, the event organizer's adrenaline level dropped again and the first guests arrived. Then the next message of doom arrived from the kitchen: "Unfortunately, we completely forgot to make the canapés. But we can put out a few nuts." Sorry, Sir Rocco, but you won't get to the top in Berlin with this kind of dilettante spirit.

These are errors of workmanship that should never happen. Period. However, if the hotel were to fail in the end because guests in this segment prefer to live in standard rooms modelled on the studio set for *Dynasty*, we would say: we take our hats off to you. At least you tried to be anything but ordinary. And that is never, ever a mistake.

CHAPTER 13

SEXY: THE BEST MANAGERS HAVE THE BEST EMPLOYEES

Austin Powers, the "Spy Who Shagged Me" in Hollywood's offbeat parody of the 1960s James Bond films, has an adversary who is as evil as he is intelligent, and who is naturally enough called Dr Evil. This bald-headed rogue in the light grey suit is never alone, but is accompanied everywhere he goes by a Lilliputian who looks exactly like his lord and master, right down to the lack of hair. Dr Evil aptly calls him Mini-Me. He is a clone, a double, a facsimile and a factotum. From the point of view of his boss, Mini-Me is the perfect subordinate.

We are absolutely certain that Mini-Me must have been hired by a professional recruiter. Maybe a head-hunter with the hourly rates of a helicopter service spent six months searching for him. Or he emerged the victor from an assessment centre that tested 800 applicants. In any case, Dr Evil and his Human Resources Director must have been immensely proud of having found exactly the right candidate in the end.

Make your own employees!

The same thing evidently occurs in quite a few companies. Somehow or other they manage to recruit exact copies of the big chief. These Mini-Mes look like the boss, dress like the boss, talk like the boss and even smell like the boss. And some time or other they inevitably also start to think just like the boss. And that is precisely the problem.

Joined the company just three months ago, and already he's a "Mini-Me"!

Harvard professor Rosabeth Moss Kanter describes this phenomenon cuttingly as "homosocial reproduction". Entrepreneurs and executives always look for the same personality traits when it comes to recruitment and advancement – the ones they themselves like. As a result, a kind of "reproduction" of the group actually does occur – through the addition of almost identical minds. Kanter found that most managers unconsciously relied on purely external features to find out who was suitable for a specific position. Ultimately, their only concern was to secure their own power by surrounding themselves with people who fitted seamlessly into the system and whom they could regard as people of their own type. During the appraisal interview, halfway through the trial period, managers then heap high praise on how fast a new recruit has acclimatized. Joined the company just three months ago, and already he's a "Mini-Me"!

There are two conflicting sayings: "Opposites attract" and "Birds of a feather flock together". Which one is true? Psychology's answer is clear: birds of a feather are attracted to each other as if by magic. Robert Sutton, a Professor at the Stanford Business School, describes this effect as follows: unconsciously, we give preference to people who are similar to us in appearance or behaviour, who went to school with us, were born in the same year or are similar to us in some other way that we find important. And we often also assess them more positively. Conversely, significant differences, regardless of how self-assured, intelligent or highly qualified the person is, unconsciously often trigger negative feelings. This leads either to subtle forms of rejection, such as avoidance of contact, or to less subtle ones, for example in the form of the decision not to hire somebody. The vast majority of people don't even notice that their feelings and decisions are being influenced in this way.

Steve Ballmer could even give the bunny from the Duracell adverts an inferiority complex.

It only remains to ask: what is actually the problem when managers surround themselves with their own lookalikes? Well, maybe you would agree with us that Communism, with its enforced conformity, wasn't really a good idea. Even though there are a few obstinate die-hards in Pyongyang who vehemently dispute this opinion. We are deeply convinced that energy always arises from clashes. Take, for example, the congenial Microsoft pairing Bill Gates and Steve Ballmer. The two men are entirely opposing personalities. Gates, who often comes across as shy, was too brainy by half even as a child and therefore had a hard life. School and sports bored him, but computers exerted an immense fascination. Steve Ballmer, in contrast, is anything but shy. In a recent article, the *FAZ* newspaper referred ironically to Ballmer as a boss who could even give the bunny from the Duracell adverts an inferiority complex. His behaviour, it said, was a cross between that of a football trainer and a televangelist.

How true! If you've ever seen the video recordings of Ballmer's appearances at staff meetings, you'll find what you saw and heard hard to forget. This hefty guy runs and jumps across the stage, gasping, in a sweat-stained shirt, hoarsely repeating four words: "I! Love! This! Company!" He can be assured of the applause of the employees present. That said, Ballmer had to undergo surgery on his vocal chords after one such appearance. It's probable that the complementary differences between these two men have gone a long way towards making Microsoft what it is today.

Let's take another congenial pair from the IT world: Sergey Brin and Larry Page, the two inventors of Internet search engine Google. Here, too, we see the same pattern as with Gates and Ballmer: Larry, the quiet, reflective Midwesterner and Sergey, the extrovert, self-confident, athletic guy from the former Soviet Union. What they have in common, however, is the characteristic of never avoiding an argument. And they demand that from their employees as well. They don't want Mini-Mes at Google, but people who think innovatively. The principle "feel free to ask awkward questions" applies there.

"He's my harshest critic. I need him desperately."

Brin and Page surround themselves with the kind of people who can be critics, who complement them. Rey More, Senior Vice President of Motorola, once described a colleague roughly as follows: "I have this radical left-winger working for me. He's my harshest critic. He tells me I am wrong. He compensates for my blind spots. I need him desperately."

That's exactly the point! If you surround yourself entirely with yes-men, bag-carriers and courtiers, you needn't be surprised if only mediocre ideas come out in the end. Really good and innovative ideas arise in an environment that not only allows differences, but actually promotes them.

SEXY

Thou shalt have no other gods before me!

"Just where do new ideas come from?" asks Nicholas Negroponte, head of the MIT Media Lab in Boston, then answers the question himself: "It's quite simple – from differences. Creativity comes from unlikely juxtapositions. The best way to maximize differences is to mix ages, cultures and disciplines".

And the reality? Many companies are so deeply incestuous that you could only tell their employees apart if they wore numbers on their backs. You can't expect much in the way of innovation from a company where more than 90 per cent of employees are the same sex, the same age, from a similar social background and with similar educational and professional careers. Even if such a company runs a really off-the-wall outdoor-team-experience-bonding-event once a year with the support of a professional trainer and always goes to a lot of trouble to hold its annual strategy meeting at really crazy venues.

Intelligence, courage and entrepreneurial thinking are not the prerogative of 48-year-old white men.

In reality, companies that try systematically to model their employee structure on a shoal of fish will come under more and more pressure. Intelligence, courage and entrepreneurial thinking are subject to normal distribution, and are not the prerogative of 48-year-old white men. The only conclusion to be drawn from this is that we should stop rewarding uniformity, adaptation and normality! Managers should not encourage homosocial reproduction, but should learn to appreciate diversity in thinking styles. How do you do that? The answer is simple: hire people who really don't fit in with you.

The problem a lot of managers have with that is obvious: first of all, such people are a pain in the neck. They get on your nerves; they have rough edges and won't take a simple "no" for an answer. Yes, it's damn hard work! And these oddballs won't fit in with a corporate culture that doesn't tolerate diversity and where independent thinking is seen as treachery. If you hire people who are different from you, but still expect them to fit in nicely, both sides are bound to be disappointed. Because these employees will be perceived as troublemakers who do nothing but disrupt business processes. They will be tolerated at best, but never promoted.

These guys get on your nerves; they have rough edges and won't take a simple "no" for an answer.

In an environment like this, the old rule once more proves true: third-rate managers hire people who are not as good as they are. Second-rate managers hire people who are as good as they are. And first-rate managers hire people who are better than they are. "Better" in this context doesn't mean that they have more management talent. But they may be more creative, more offbeat, more interesting than the boss. And that is precisely why they got the job. We cannot emphasize that point enough: the core task of managers is *not* to develop innovations themselves. Their job is to build an organization that is capable of continuously producing innovative ideas and reinventing itself over and over again. In other words, their contribution consists of *creating the environment* for these first-rate employees; it is not their job to invent the content. And that also means that the bosses have to do everything in their power to create an environment in which people can fully live their talents.

Nevertheless, many managers are repeatedly – and wrongly – tempted to suppress this very principle with all their might, more or less according to the commandment: thou shalt have no other gods before me. The fear that someone could steal their show is simply too great. That, however, is insane.

Can you imagine any publisher in the world being annoyed if one of his authors were to win the Nobel Prize for Literature? Just because he didn't write the books himself? Not on your life! He will be popping the champagne corks because his wildest dreams have come true. Or do you think Frank Rijkaard, when he was the FC Barcelona trainer, sat weeping in a corner when his Brazilian soccer star Ronaldinho was once more voted footballer of the year?

Why do managers in business find it so hard to apply this principle? And it is quite simple, after all: you hire a group of intelligent people and stay out of their hair until they ask you for help. The reason is obvious: if you tell them what to do, you'll be laying chains on their creativity and ruining their motivation. Alberto Alessi, CEO of the Italian design factory of the same name, once said in an interview with the *Zeit* weekly newspaper: "I myself do not work as a designer, and I don't do any drawing, either. My task is to find new designers and help them to realize their inspirations. A kind of mediator between the designer's ideas and the customer's dreams, that's how I would describe myself." Mr Alessi, you've got the message!

Multicultural to the outside world – monotone inside

Some companies do pledge allegiance to the notion of diversity, on paper at least. They are fond of placing full-page ads in leading newspapers, touting their efforts to promote diversity, including the obligatory photo of a variegated bunch of employees grouped around a conference table – including, naturally, the obligatory female employee of Asian origin. And of course she has to be accompanied by the colleague whose African roots even a Polar bear would recognize. The tenor is performance through passion, that's all that counts, origin and skin colour do not matter. Sadly, we experience this "corporate diversity" thing very often as a serious case of dual morality.

One of our friends had the misfortune to discover this when he responded to a completely off-the-wall, unconventional job advertisement with an equally insane application. He was promptly invited to an interview. When he got there, they explained that he had only been invited so that the company could see for themselves exactly what kind of nutter would send in an application like that. Because, of course, the supercreative company with the offbeat ad had expected a totally classic application. Great.

He saw it as enriching that not all his employees had the same orientation as him.

We don't think you should focus your selection procedures solely on lunatics in strange clothing, with offbeat attitudes and weird behaviour. We do think, however, that a company's employees, including those at management level, should reflect the market outside. And this market does not just include 55-year-old white males, but also young, coloured, lesbian, alternative-music-loving customers. What do these customers have in common with the male, 55-year-old manager caste? N-o-t-h-i-n-g!

Companies that still subscribe to uniformity, adjustment and normality must understand that they won't be able to develop ideas that are in any way attractive to their customers if they take that attitude. It isn't a question of bringing these managers closer to their customers by means of surgical or other drastic interventions. The solution is rather to integrate this diversity actively into their own companies.

Here's an example we experienced in person at a major European

116

lifestyle company. The chief executive, a very distinguished man in his early sixties, mentioned in the course of conversation with some embarrassment but not without pride that he had recently hired someone who had a "bit of a different orientation". In other words, the new hire was gay. Now, in view of the fact that there's hardly any major European city these days with a heterosexual mayor, it was astonishing enough that anyone could be embarrassed about that. Yet at least the man was thinking along the right lines, and taking action accordingly. He hired someone to compensate for the blind spots that inevitably occur in a homogeneous management team.

Diversity is a product of strength

How do you find employees who are not clones of you, and who will help your company to progress because of their very difference? It's dead simple: you become a magnet. In a magnet, a strong positive pole attracts strong negative poles. A strong personality exerts an enormous attraction for different, complementary personalities.

You could put it like this: excellent leaders are attractive. Everyone wants to work for them, be around them, be part of their network. As a rule, such managers don't have a problem with conflict. The best ones need opposition, people with whom some friction occurs. As a corrective, and because their own creativity demands it.

One route to this goal is "reverse socialization". Normally, managers and colleagues try to make new employees conform as quickly as possible and bring them in line with the corporate mentality. In some companies, it almost borders on brain-washing; at others it operates more subtly, for example through praise of everything that somebody does "as though he had been with the company for ten years". Strong leaders turn this principle on its head and ask new staff to teach something to the veterans in the company. The old ones have to listen to the new ones; this means that the former are forced to look at themselves in the mirror and to invite criticism of the status quo.

Taking this idea to its logical conclusion, the boss should not ask a new employee at the end of the trial period whether he has acclimatized well. No, the question should be quite different: "What still surprises you? How could we solve our problems with ideas that you have learnt elsewhere?" Very few do this kind of thing. But particularly because very few do it, it offers an enormous opportunity: you can learn a lot from employees who are not – yet – inured to the company's practices.

CHAPTER 14

THE DIFFERENCE: FIRST, GOOD TEAMS HAVE A COMPELLING CAUSE AND SECOND, THEY HAVE A LEADER

In the mid-1970s, IBM, "Big Blue", was the undisputed world market leader in anything to do with computers. Remember, by the way, that in those days a computer was not a neat little unit that would fit on any desk. At that time, computers were the size of wardrobes – but you could do less with them than any 14-year-old would expect these days from his mobile phone.

At that time, a team of five engineers in the German IBM office in Mannheim had a brilliant idea for a new product that wasn't available anywhere on the market. They wanted to develop business software that would help companies to run recurring resource planning and control processes more simply and efficiently. They had the vision of a kind of standard business program that could be sold to any company anywhere in the world.

The idea was shot down. Too far-fetched, not in line with the core business.

The team of developers presented the idea to their bosses at IBM. They rejected it. The idea was shot down. Too far-fetched, not in line with the core business. The engineers' time would be better employed in improving existing products; after all, there was still plenty of scope left in the German market. In that second, the team experienced an epiphany: for them, IBM was history, effective immediately. Even though the best minds were fighting over jobs at Big Blue at that time. The five were so convinced of their idea that they wouldn't allow anyone to stand in their way.

The names of those engineers were Claus Wellenreuther, Hans-Werner Hector, Klaus Tschira, Dietmar Hopp and Hasso Plattner. They left IBM and set up a small company with the desperately boring name "Systeme, Anwendungen, Produkte in der Datenverarbeitung" (Systems, Applications and Products in Data Processing). Under the acronym SAP, this company is now famous as the world market leader in standard enterprise software. The idea whose potential IBM completely failed to recognize formed the basis of the biggest success story for a new German company since World War II.

It's pointless to plan a route if you don't know where you're going

So what motivated SAP's founders to create a software firm in Germany, in the 1970s? The answer: passion and the shared objective to develop standard application software for real-time business processing. An idea that was brilliant in both technical and business terms. They were ready to give their all and risk their all to develop and market it. Disappointment with the old guard that had met them only with incomprehension fed their constructive anger and spurred them on all the more.

By the way, Bill Gates had tried to sell his young enterprise Microsoft with its team to IBM for $30 million in the 1970s. Big Blue turned him down politely on the grounds that neither he nor any of his 30 employees had the qualifications required for a job with IBM. The rejection ultimately proved to be a blessing, because whether Bill Gates and Steve Ballmer would have done terribly well as line managers at IBM is extremely questionable.

But we are *not* interested here in IBM's disastrous tendency to throw away mega opportunities. We are interested in highly effective and successful teams. One of the crucial success factors is a strong shared objective. This is what welds a collection of experts who happen to be working on the same thing into a real team. It does not necessarily have to be a lofty goal wreathed in emotion to produce outstanding results. But even if the matter in hand is only to market Plenty kitchen paper, the team responsible needs a tangible objective, a shared idea, a common passion.

Merely earning money is not sufficient as the compelling cause.

Merely earning money is not sufficient as the compelling cause that drives a great team. It needs something to give it direction and a sense of pride. However mundane a company's products or services may be, they have to be imbued with the sense of an overarching purpose. You don't achieve that with the blanket distribution of sweet sentiments from the PR department's treasury of stock phrases. This sense has to come from that part of a person that longs to make the world a slightly better place. Eric Schmidt, the third boss at the head of Google together with Sergey Brin and Larry Page, once said in an interview that they tried to recruit people who strove for a better world, and who didn't work at Google because of the money, but because they could make something happen. These people are welded together by a shared m-i-s-s-i-o-n. That makes this company really strong.

In order for everyone to be convinced that a journey is worth all the trouble, they have to be clear about the destination. The shared goal is not static, nor is it enough to align yourself to it only once. Enthusiasm for the thing that has brought people together has to be constantly kept alive.

Researchers have discovered that goal orientation plays a particularly striking role in high-performance teams such as fire services, rescue services and special police task forces. The absolute will to put out a fire, save a seriously injured person or free a hostage forges very different people together in teams where every move is honed to perfection. Nobody has to stop and think before acting, everything simply fits together and the operation works like clockwork. Hierarchies have virtually no role to play. Teams in companies can learn a lot from that.

Few things are as characteristic of everyday working life in Germany as banding together.

When we listen to people in various companies, we often get the feeling that the shared objectives are diffuse at best. People are a team because it just feels so nice to be a team. And because they don't want to leave anyone out.

Co-determined failure is preferred to tightly managed success

Herbert Henzler, the former head of McKinsey Europe, writes in one of his books: "Being German means being a crowd." That's our experience, too. Few things are as characteristic of everyday working life in Germany as banding together. Work groups in German companies typically don't just include those immediately affected by an issue or experts in the subject, but everyone who has some interest in the topic, who would like to have a say, or who would simply like to see a few familiar faces again. Some companies with a strange sense of humour even regard this as their "democratic" corporate culture. To them, co-determination is when everyone talks at once and nothing is decided.

One of us was once a consultant on a project at a large German airport. The consulting team simply couldn't get going because it was an unwritten law at the state-owned airport operating company that everybody – literally everybody – who was involved in the slightest – literally the slightest – way in the project had to attend every – literally every – discussion.

Co-determination is when everyone talks at once and nothing is decided.

People just needed the feel-good factor that nothing was decided without them and that they knew at first hand what was going on in the project. And after the second cup of coffee, of course, they really brightened up, interfered in things that had nothing to do with them and made suggestions on topics they didn't have a clue about. These people are clearly confusing a well-intentioned duty of information with a genuine value contribution.

Leading is more than moderating

It just isn't enough when teams can work together somehow or other. They also need a leader. That leader isn't a person who gives orders that have to be carried out meticulously. He is a person who embodies the shared objective of the team.

Some time ago we saw a documentary about the Berlin Philharmonic Orchestra. There's a scene in it where one of the orchestra's musicians visits a class of youngsters in their early school years and explains why the orchestra actually needs a conductor. Of course, he couldn't tell the children any esoteric stuff about the conductor embodying the spirit of the greater whole or whatever. But he gave a very practical reason. An orchestra is so big and so loud that the violin at the front right cannot possibly hear the harp at the back left. The orchestra needs a conductor because somebody has to have the overview. What musicians don't need is someone telling them how to play the violin or the harp.

Somebody has to have the lighthouse view and see the big picture.

This idea can easily be transferred to business teams. Somebody has to see the big picture. When one of us was employed at an international consultancy, they worked for a boss who had this lighthouse view. He never wanted to know the details. And he never gave instructions in the style of "Do this" or "Clarify that". Instead, his contributions came in the form of the finest understatement: "You may want to consider …", and he always hit the nail on the head. Every time, he saw something that we were too familiar with the project to notice. And by doing so, he set the bar a little bit higher every time.

Straight out, then: we do not advocate setting goals for teams as if they were special-needs children. The problem is that it is so easy to under-stretch teams. Just think of all those adult education groups where the achievement of the smallest goals is acclaimed with a whoop and a holler as an epochal event. Ellen has managed to say "Good evening" aloud in the group. Fantastic, a new stage in life has begun. For Ellen.

We think we have to set the bar a little bit higher these days. And the team leader has an important role here, because he spurs people on to perform by always defining the objectives a little bit more ambitiously than the team would have done of its own accord.

In one of his books, management author and Stanford professor Robert Sutton relates an anecdote about film director Francis Ford Coppola which demonstrates beautifully how far real team leaders will go to keep their teams on the ball, even in difficult situations. The filming of *Apocalypse Now* proved extremely tough. The location work was on the brink of descending into chaos. At that point, script author John Milius appointed himself the spokesman of those who thought there was no point in going on. However, Milius was anything but comfortable having a one-on-one interview with Coppola. He said he felt like a general going to tell Hitler in 1944 that the fuel stocks were exhausted. But Coppola broke the ice and managed to inspire Milius to total enthusiasm. And he promised that *Apocalypse Now* would be the first film ever to win a Nobel Prize. That, of course, was sheer nonsense, but Coppola was so convincing that Milius came out of the interview and yelled: "We're going to win the war! We don't need any fuel." Of course, they only had to make a war film and not win a real war, but in the end it was a triumph for Coppola and his team. The film wasn't nominated for the Nobel Prize, but for eight Oscars instead. It ultimately received three.

CHAPTER 15

DUMPING BALLAST: TO THE SCRAPHEAP WITH STATUS SYMBOLS AND FORMAL AUTHORITY

The Palace of Versailles. St Peter's Basilica in Rome. Ludwig II's romantic castles in Bavaria. Highly impressive, particularly for Asian and American tourists. They're the most memorable status symbols of the powerful ones of the past. They've endured through the years and now attract many millions of marvelling people every year. What magnificence. What glory. What power they must have had to make these buildings possible. If you know something about European history, however, you'll be aware that all of these magnificent buildings were constructed when the power systems behind them were already going downhill.

St Peter's Basilica in Rome was built at a time when the Reformation was already knocking on the door. Yet the Renaissance popes ignored all the warning signs, preferring to invest in marble, gold and magnificent frescoes. In Paris, just as the *ancien régime* was applying the last piece of gold leaf to Versailles, the guillotine was being oiled. And insane Bavarian king Ludwig II's romantic castles did not ultimately prevent him from drowning in Lake Starnberg.

Ego crutches

Ancient history? Yes and no. This type of bombastic self-display still exists today. It's just that it's no longer commissioned by popes and monarchs, but by companies or their top management instead. Yet just as in the Rome, Versailles or Bavaria of old, all the signs today indicate that the corporate princes who put up wonderful buildings as monuments to themselves are the ones with their best days behind them. Now, this raises the heretical question of whether companies weaken because they devote their entire attention to self-display, or whether they devote themselves to magnificence because they have nothing better to do any more. Whatever the case, so long as exciting discoveries or big leaps forward are being made, no one has time to plan opulent headquarters.

In the mid-1980s, an ambitious manager came to power at the traditional Daimler-Benz AG corporation. Edzard Reuter had an integrated technology group as his vision. Cars, lorries and buses would still be part of it, but aeroplanes, moon rockets, refrigerators, satellites and tanks would be added. Reuter's telegenic small-screen appearances taught the Germans a new word: synergy. And thanks to this grandiose idea, the group was undoubtedly set to be the biggest, most powerful and most prestigious in the world.

Now, it was naturally beneath the dignity of the managers of an emerging high-tech Mecca for the 21st century to have their offices in the middle of a car factory. Possibly even to have to pass through the same factory gate as oil-smeared production line workers. No, they had to have a new headquarters as soon as possible. In an idyllic suburban location in the Swabian metropolis of Stuttgart, a building arose that was architecturally dead boring, but very fancy. A heap of giant Lego blocks scattered across a field. Edzard Reuter raved about the "campus atmosphere". The integrated synergetic global group and its Harvard on the river Neckar.

Edzard Reuter's synergies led to a series of gigantic flops which plunged the group into a deep crisis. And Reuter's successor Juergen Schrempp described the unpopular prestigious building pitilessly as "Bullshit Castle". Daimler survived the Reuter era, just as the Catholic Church survived the Reformation. Nevertheless, Bullshit Castle was sold in 2006. The top management moved back to Untertuerkheim to those same oil-smeared production line workers, who are really the roots and the backbone of the car producer. The concrete, steel and glass status symbol landed on the scrapheap of the company's history. And verily we say unto you: that's where it belonged.

How different, in contrast, is the atmosphere in young, innovative and fast growing companies, where people sit among packing cases in half-furnished offices. Who needs pictures on the wall or books on the shelf? The main thing is that the computer works and somebody takes care of the appointments. After all, the people are there to implement ideas, and not to impress somebody or other. What's more, they have absolutely no time to click their way for hours through the online configurator for the new company car in order to decide between an aluminium-inlaid steering wheel or one with a wooden rim.

There are no passion implants, and you can't buy visions at Harrods.

Of course, not all companies can remain eternal start-ups. But nevertheless, the question is: do they focus on the real thing or on the symbolism? Do managers circle round and round themselves, or do they do everything in their power to make visions come true? Against this background it soon becomes clear that power regalia are a thing of the day before yesterday and can be junked. Managers who need status symbols are showing initiated observers their insecurity. Fear. They don't have the self-confidence to lead people only through what they are and through leadership by example. That's why they need ego crutches.

But all those Blackberries, big limousines, private jets, Blancpain watches, Vertu mobile phones and Barcelona armchairs are no substitute for heart and brains. There are no passion implants, and you can't buy visions at Harrods. Real leaders walk without crutches. They just set out on their journey and others follow them, because both the leaders themselves and the path they're taking are attractive. You're not the boss because you have an extra window in your office or a higher back to your desk chair, but because you're more enthusiastic and courageous than any of the others.

Back in the first half of the twentieth century, the legendary Bavarian cabaret performer Karl Valentin picked up on the way people change with a minimal increase in their authority and the associated symbols of office. He tells the story of a Munich tram conductor who had to weave his way between the passengers, day in and day out. He knew the regulars, the newcomers, the notorious fare-dodgers. He gave a friendly pat on the shoulder here, a punch in the side there. The passengers liked him.

One day, however, some boss of his had the idea of placing the conductor on a platform. When they got on, the passengers had to file past him and show or buy their tickets. From that day forth the previously so-friendly tram conductor changed. Now he was higher up in both the literal and metaphorical senses of the word, and he immediately started ordering people to move along faster or have the correct change ready.

In the production hall, they call it the "big cheese bouncer".

This phenomenon is just as current now as in Karl Valentin's day. The minute someone is promoted to head of department or is granted high-level signing powers, access to his office is barred by a secretary. There is even a separate lift to take the management board members up to the top floor. In the production hall, they call it the "big cheese bouncer".

Another highly popular topic is the size of a person's office. This is strictly based on the occupant's position. When you're on level seventeen or lower in the hierarchy, you're assigned a rabbit hutch. But once you've arrived, a real office will be waiting for you. So the rule is that the most senior person, that is, the one who is least often in the office, gets the biggest room with the best view and the best light. The poor infantry, the ones who are there round the clock every day, get the office cell looking onto the kitchen.

But watch out for what happens in such companies if they're ever faced with major restructuring. You can guarantee that for months on end there will be no other subject under discussion but the sizes of the new offices compared with the old ones. If anyone's square footage is to be reduced, verbal punch-ups or worse are the inevitable consequence.

Only those who can't help themselves make a display of power

Of course, the more subtle signs of power, which can be communicated perfectly with the help of office furnishings, are particularly seductive. These painstakingly selected artefacts are nothing but a carefully compiled collection of visual messages: the first of these messages is that the office occupant was once a real top athlete. Take note of golf balls cast in Plexiglas cubes and framed team photos. A propos photos, they can of course also be used to send a second important message: anyone who thinks pictures are just an attractive wall decoration is vastly mistaken. It is not about what's on them, but about the person *with whom* our executive is shown in the pictures ... thanks to digital technology, it is no problem at all these days to make your own photo with the Pope, Bill Clinton, or the Dalai Lama look perfectly authentic.

If you don't have any snapshots with Bill Gates-Clinton-Murray or Papa Ratzi, you can use another trick if necessary: plaster your office with large-scale modern art. By doing that, you show not only that you can afford such pictures, but also that you are at the forefront of the times and even know which way up they should be hung.

Another very important accessory is books. You can really

learn something from the academics here: you will never find a photo of a scientist in the newspaper where he or she is not sitting in front of an impressive wall of books. Maybe that's why you could always see a book-case behind George Bush when he held his State of the Nation addresses? But was it actually his own bookcase, or was he just visiting the Washington National Library? Oh, well, we suppose we're straying a bit from the point there. At any rate, he didn't make the same mistake as Cora Schumacher (wife of former F1 driver Ralf Schumacher) when she dictated to the pen of high-brow weekly newspaper *Welt am Sonntag*: "as far as books are concerned, I don't get around much from the reading point of view." No, of course a real executive reads a lot of serious books, which decorate the office shelves. The fact that the pages of most of these thick tomes are virginally untouched may easily escape the eye of the unpractised observer.

I am so important, I never have time!

Another particularly ingenious status symbol is having privileged access to information that is withheld from other employees. Who is CC'd in on the really important emails and who isn't? Who is the first to be initiated by the chief executive into the still-confidential strategy? The permitted maximum dose of information increases in many companies exactly in line with the size of the office. It reminds us of the film *Total Recall* with Arnold Schwarzenegger. There's this scene where a person starts to tell his boss: "But I thought …" and is rudely interrupted: "Who told you to 'think'? I don't give you enough information to 'think'!"

That's precisely what happens every day in thousands of companies. When information is equated with power, granting access to it would be the equivalent of a loss of power. Sharing information with others robs managers of the pleasant feeling of having power over their employees. Intelligent companies take a completely different approach. They are creating a democracy of information that makes information accessible to everyone, for example via the intranet. Consequently the employees can act in the interests of the company.

"Who told you to 'think'? I don't give you enough information to 'think'!"

Making information available is not only a question of technology, by the way. The necessary hardware, software and network environment has long been in place almost everywhere. The actual barrier lies in corporate culture that rewards information hoarding. So long as vertical, functional and cultural barriers are instrumentalized and maintained for power plays, so long as rigid job definitions paralyze employees and curiosity is punished in Draconian style, creative potential will be wasted in a way that is nothing short of foolish.

Of course, there are always excuses to justify information control. Only a fundamental change in managers' thinking will make them understand that sharing information is a catalyst for innovation and greater individual responsibility on the part of every employee. An executive once told us in a discussion of this subject: "We have the tools to do it. But do we have the will as well?"

It doesn't have to be that way: personality as a status symbol

Things are changing, however. A new generation of managers is determined to do things differently. These executives love what they do. They vibrate with energy and infect their colleagues and employees with it. Dietrich Mateschitz, the founder and CEO of Red Bull, says he only works three days a week. That is evidently enough to be sensationally successful. That's cool. And it should make all the other oh-so-busy executives who flourish their full-to-bursting diaries in everyone's faces think twice.

A leader is someone who has followers.

At Hewlett-Packard in Boeblingen, a city in southwest Germany, the bosses don't even have their own offices. They have desks in an open-plan room. The innovative and successful US company Gore combats the traditional signs of status and hierarchy with a principle that is both simple and effective: "a leader is someone who has followers". This principle is brilliant because it's precisely the crucial question that any boss should be asking himself repeatedly: Would my employees work with me voluntarily if they really had the choice?

People who have changed the world have never needed any status symbols. According to our information, Mother Teresa didn't have a business card that said "Nobel Laureate" in seven languages. Gandhi didn't wear Budapest shoes or a Patek Philippe watch. We once met the Dalai Lama – he really doesn't make a big to-do about himself. Poet Vaclav Havel had never owned an expensive suit in his life. As state President, he led first Czechoslovakia and later the Czech Republic into a new era. You don't need formal authority and you certainly don't need status symbols to start something new. What you do need is a compelling vision for the future that inspires people to follow voluntarily.

Mother Teresa didn't have a business card that said "Nobel Laureate" in seven languages.

Companies that are managed by true leaders naturally do have symbols as well. But they are the kind that express belonging more than status. We don't mean the bad habit to be found (particularly in US companies) of showering employees with mugs, T-shirts, pennants or desk signs prominently displaying either the company logo or icky phrases like "You are the most important person in this company".

Symbols can be rituals, such as the homemade curry-Wurst sausage that is served every Tuesday lunchtime at the VW factory in Wolfsburg. The sausages are eaten by gateman and CEO alike. That creates a sense of identity and bonds people together. And such rituals can never be ordained from above; they just arise over time in line with the corporate culture.

When we say that status symbols belong on the scrapheap, we don't mean that successful entrepreneurs and top managers should give up consumption entirely and practise the asceticism of an Indian saddhu. Quite the contrary. If an entrepreneur fulfils the dream of his youth and buys a Porsche or a Mercedes SL to drive around in at weekends, that has nothing to do with status symbols per se. It has to do with fun and joie de vivre. It is only when the top manager's limousine is parked two metres from the main entrance, blocking the way for the rest of the staff, that it no longer comes down to "enjoying driving", but to compulsive differentiation. And that, in turn, has nothing whatsoever to do with success or fun.

CHAPTER 16

CHANGE OF PERSPECTIVE: FROM SUPERIOR CRAFTSMAN TO ENABLER

Henry Ford is supposed to have once said: "Why is it that whenever I ask for a pair of hands a brain comes attached?" What a nuisance. After all, a real manager knows himself what should be done. The only problem is that unfortunately you can't be everywhere at once. How impractical.

That's a rough description of how management was perceived at the beginning of the modern industrial society. The symbol of the first evolutionary stage of management is the *hand*.

Historically, this perception of management is easy to understand. Industry developed from individual crafts. And in crafts, the master is the best craftsman. Consequently, the master has the say in his workshop.

In small manufacturing operations, the situation is normally no different from that which existed two hundred years ago: "In my company, the apprentice has to learn his craft first. And it will take years before he is a true master craftsman." The challenge for many bosses seems to be that they simply cannot let go. They are convinced that nobody does it better than they do. Which is why they can't stop themselves from constantly meddling in other people's work.

Hands, head and heart – H³ for executives

The symbol of the second evolutionary stage of management is the *head*. In the emerging knowledge society, bosses have realized that they are no longer just looking for the most diligent hands, but the best heads. And the best head is the boss's, of course. This type of boss has outgrown the role of best craftsman and become best schoolmaster. The boss is the one who knows better, who wonders how he can educate his employees. These types of bosses believe that they already have all the answers as to how their company should run. More or less according to the motto: what made me personally successful can't be all that wrong for other people. And so management becomes adult education. One of the magic words here is "motivation". That is often synonymous with "manipulation", because it is mainly about external control. The employees have a new motto emailed to them every day to improve their morale, such as "I will become one per cent better every day" or "We're not interested in the problem, but the solution". And to strengthen general self-esteem, the word "workforce" is deleted from all internal communications and replaced by "associates" who are "highly motivated", "take on responsibility" without being asked, "leave beaten tracks", have "a sense of humour" and "take over responsibility". But so that the whole thing doesn't get completely out of hand, there is the second magic phrase – "personnel development". Here, employees are bridled once more and have it drummed into them – in a number of intensive seminars – how they can make their own thinking, behaviour and attitudes match the company's needs.

To strengthen general self-esteem, the word "workforce" is deleted from all internal communications.

We could hardly believe our eyes when we read recently in the German business magazine *Wirtschaftswoche* about a new trend. Companies were running assessment centres, actively supported by a big-name management consultancy, not just to select personnel, but also to assess the soft skills of middle managers. Is marketing manager Smith really a team player? Is financial manager Jones sufficiently assertive?

What on earth is that supposed to mean? Do bosses need assessment centres to find out whether their people are team players, or assert themselves? Let's face it, noticing these things really is a core task for any boss! Or do your employees work in a vacuum to which you are totally, really absolutely totally, oblivious? There are evidently managers out there who find it too much of an effort to engage with their employees, and who are firmly convinced that such trivia will only distract them from real management tasks. What a joke!

There are companies where all new graduate recruits get the same development plan handed out to them on their first day. The plan plainly identifies the drum to which they are ultimately intended to march. After all, bosses and personnel developers have to carry out their statutory duty of education. They do have that duty, don't they? At all events, a lot of them behave as though they do. And so an entire profession makes an extremely good living from moulding well-behaved employees to be even more comparable, adaptable and interchangeable than they already are.

But people are not machines that can be controlled at the touch of a button or moulded any way you like. You can't develop them; they'll do that themselves or not at all.

The boss of the future is an "enabler" instead of a craftsman or a schoolmaster.

The era of the hand is over. The era of the head is just drawing to a close. And what comes next? The symbol of the third and, for the time being, last stage of evolution in management is the heart. Business is about emotions. No, we're not talking about group hugs. We mean passion. The passion of people who want to achieve something, who want to make something of their lives, who want to discover their talents and get the best out of them. Managers who passionately care about their employees. Employees who passionately care about their customers and products. The boss of the future is an "enabler" instead of a craftsman or a schoolmaster. He understands how to create an environment in which people can develop their full potential. He gets the greatest talents on board and makes sure that they can make a difference at work.

Control is good, trust is better

In a lot of companies it is considered quite sufficient for someone to prove himself in his current role in order to be deemed fit for higher duties and responsibilities. So far, so bad. Because, unfortunately, there is no scientifically proven correlation between technical expertise and the aptitude to be a manager. We are all aware of the Peter Principle. Your top salespeople may not necessarily be the best managers. Or highly qualified engineers with brilliant ideas may prove to be pale technocrats when they take the R&D director's chair. The best managers today are not distinguished by technical or functional expertise, but by the fact that they possess leadership skills and open up the opportunity for these people to give their best.

That is the essence of leadership today. And it should not be confused with management. Management means solving problems more or less creatively, and improving an existing thing to some degree. Real leaders, in contrast, challenge the status quo. In this sense, leadership means opening up new horizons of possibility. In addition to a great deal of energy and excellent knowledge of human nature, leaders chiefly need three things: first, *trust* in others; second, *willingness to delegate power*; and third, a clear *direction*.

Real leaders challenge the status quo.

"Trust: The Best Way to Manage" – yes, of course, all managers have heard that phrase. After all, executives read books too, and nobody wants to be limping behind the *Zeitgeist*. "Trust and mutual respect are the foundations of our success" hangs on the wall in the conference room, written in beautiful calligraphy and framed. The strange thing is that in a lot of companies this trust is expressed in a 200-page manual in which the management sets forth its entire approach to major projects in minute detail, so that everything remains nicely under control. Yet Lenin's "trust is good, control is better" is really the thinking that dominates a lot of minds on the management floors. And not the wall-mounted sayings.

"That's okay", might be your first reaction, "our company abolished manuals like that way back in 1955." That's nice for you, but control can be exercised in a more subtle mode. Take personal decision-making power, for instance. If a company grants its staff complete freedom in all decisions up to a maximum amount of €5.99, you don't have to be a psychoanalyst to make incisive deductions about the management's notion of leadership. It is classic self-fulfilling prophecy: for fear of not being able to trust their staff, companies create a climate of supervision and control in which at some point breaking rules really becomes the only way for an employee to regain his independence and self-esteem.

You could put it this way: if the management team is not prepared to grant its employees freedom and trust, it can't expect these people to take on any kind of responsibility.

It sounds so wonderfully simple. But as with most wonderfully simple things in life, it gets a little bit more complicated when people try to implement it. Let's assume we want to en*trust* a project to a staff member. Easier said than done. That's why some executives find a way that in their eyes is much more intelligent: they don't delegate decision-making authority, only responsibility. In other words, they delegate the possibility of failure. Yet the prerequisite for the genuine delegation of a task or an entire project is trust. And that's where it gets complicated. Delegating work is always a good idea – but accepting the possibility of mistakes or even failure, who wants to do that?

That's just where the body is buried: while the traditional management focus is on control, enablers concentrate on building a readiness to take risks and showing their employees how to manage risks intelligently – making well-informed and thoroughly considered bets that will pay off for the company.

Leadership begins on the far side of power

But stop right there! Halt! Not every employee can handle the maximum of freedom. That's true, we've no wish to deny it. The amount of freedom that individuals or teams are granted has to match their capabilities. And assessing that amount and adjusting it accordingly is a leadership task. Of course you can get it wrong. That happens from time to time. But it's our only chance. Leaders have to learn to live with the risk of making a wrong assessment. The alternative would be a bureaucratic monster, a gigantic implementation mechanism that meticulously checks to see that every rule is followed, and where ultimately all talent suffocates. We hope you don't find this description all too familiar …

Let's talk briefly about power.

Let's talk briefly about power. Enablers need no formal power. Instead, they rely on their own natural authority, which comes from within and does not have to be polished to a shine every day on their platinum business card. Here's a small example: when one of us was still working for a big management consultancy, they carried out one of their first consulting engagements in a manufacturing company. A real one, with shift work, huge factory halls and the noise of machines. It was a major restructuring project. In view of the task at hand, it was really no wonder that the employees gave the consulting team a fairly frosty reception. Their opinion wasn't very flattering: snotty consultants who don't have a clue but always know better. These guys with their golden cufflinks who never get their hands dirty. Middle management and the levels below didn't want any changes ordained from above in any way, shape or form, and they made that clear straight away.

In this situation, our project leader had a brilliant idea. Even before the first official day of the engagement, our whole team turned up in production at four o'clock in the morning. With no grey suits or consultant's attitude. Our job was to talk to the people in the factory, and listen to them. We sat with the workers in the lunchrooms and got them to tell us about their worries. We listened patiently in the canteen to what had to finally change in this place. The results were tremendous. Suddenly, they were on the consultants' side.

Mind you, we were deeply convinced that our project made sense. We weren't trying to pull the wool over anyone's eyes. But if we had played the card of the formal power vested in us by the executive board to implement the project we would undoubtedly have run up against a brick wall and achieved nothing. We hadn't a chance until we gave the clear signal: we're not here to get a kick out of our own power, but to support you in using your full capabilities.

Let's repeat that point, because it is so vital: enablers do not need any formal command, they rely on the power that comes from within. They understand that no individual, no group, no boss knows the exact road to the future. But they also know that leadership means clearing obstacles out of the way and being champions of change. One person has to have the courage to go first. He breaks through smugness. He stirs things up. But he also knows how to communicate a clear vision of the future.

Enablers rely on the power that comes from within.

For this purpose, it's essential to give employees a sense of direction. When we touch on this subject, everyone always sits there and nods. Yes, of course, direction, goals and stuff. Okay, okay. We work on that all the time. Why on earth are they bothering to mention it? To illustrate our point, we ask executives to agree to a little experiment. They are to imagine us going into their company and choosing ten people at random – from any department, any floor, any job. Then let's assume that we ask each of these employees the following questions: What are your company's goals? What is the special and unique thing about your company – from your customers' point of view?

Then we ask the executives: "Would we get the same answer from all the ten people?" That's the 64-thousand-dollar question, and it's often a real eye-opener. Because that is the point at which some managers, provided they are honest, have to admit to themselves that the employees' answer would probably be something like "I don't know" or "I'm not sure".

In other companies we would no doubt get an answer. Unfortunately, however, the answers would differ widely depending on which department and which area of the company we were talking to.

And let's go a step further: let's assume that we also ask: "What about the compatibility of personal goals and company goals?" What answers would we get from these ten randomly selected people? The managers can only answer that for themselves. And the same applies to you as a reader. But whatever the answer may be, we are convinced that an imperfect picture of the goals that is generally accepted and supported is more important to the company's performance than a supposedly perfect vision consisting of abstract waffle that no one believes in.

The manager who leads with heart and passion is not a nice, avuncular figure in a comfy tweed jacket, but often a merciless driver.

Successful organizations have a common understanding of their goals, strategies, priorities and direction. That seems a simple principle that people quickly agree to. But put it to the test. Are the goals commonly understood throughout the organization? In many cases, you'll be surprised by the wide divergence between the staff's assumptions and understanding of the organization's objectives, and those of management, as well as those of colleagues on the same level. The result is an organization that is working hard and getting nowhere.

Reflecting on the contents of this chapter, some readers might think that the leader of the future is a nice, avuncular figure in a comfy tweed jacket or a kind-hearted auntie who pours green tea for her visitors. We don't mean that at all. On the contrary, the leader with heart and passion is often a merciless driver. He's not like a guru in his ashram where everybody loves one another. He's not about Yin and Yang. He's more like a choreographer who drives his dance company hard and sometimes shouts at them and makes them jump to it. Not because he is domineering. But because he fights passionately to make his ensemble stand on its own two feet in self-confident, masterly fashion when the curtain goes up on the first night and for every performance thereafter.

CHAPTER 17

WE CAN DO IT DIFFERENTLY: WORK SMART, NOT HARD

We subscribe to the newsletter of a fairly well-known German communication trainer. One day, we read something extremely interesting in it: the man is currently trying to kick the habit of sleeping. Or rather, he is reducing his sleep systematically. And he recommends that everyone else follow his example. His logic is razor-sharp: if you sleep half an hour less per day – this is the starting dose of the sleep withdrawal drug – you will gain 23 additional 8-hour days every year. Think of all the things you can do with this extra time! Earn a lot more money and do and enjoy a lot more things as well. But that's only the beginning. If you actually manage to sleep a whole hour less than before, you will gain an unbelievable 46 days a year. If you reach the age of 80, you will have lived ten years longer (we should check that with a mathematician, but no matter).

Will the time come when he can't bear the thought of having to sleep at all?

He makes no bones in his newsletter about the fact that the training is damned hard. Every morning when it is still dark and quiet outside, the author subjects himself to renewed torture. But he has discovered a way to outsmart himself. He writes his sleeping time down meticulously every day, and by doing so gives himself a permanent guilty conscience. Every minute slept is a minute lost! Under this kind of pressure, he has now trained himself down to an average of 6.6 hours of sleep. The next target in his sights is 6.2 hours. Will the time come when he can't bear the thought of having to sleep at all?

People who work too hard are diligent, but unproductive

Weaning yourself off sleep is perhaps the ultimate logical conclusion for workaholics. In many places, the old principle still applies that the most competent managers and the best employees are those who work round the clock. Or at least those who strive to get as close as possible to that ideal. Although it's quite clear that the longer someone works, the less he gets done, this is the yarn from which the modern heroic sagas are spun. "Incredible", colleagues whisper during a chance meeting in the corridor, "Smithers has been working for 20 hours now. Non-stop." No problem: with the right stretching exercises, working days can easily be extended to 36 hours, and with rock-hard training you can even dramatically reduce your number of visits to the toilet.

You can forget "time management", that old stalwart of the self-help books.

No, no, we're by no means advocating a paradise for lazy so-and-sos. And we're not talking about the nationwide introduction of the 32.5-hour week either. The point is that those employees who put out the light every night should not be considered the best ones.

It's like this: if you work longer hours, you naturally structure your day differently, as well. Please don't try to tell us that you manage to keep your energy at peak during the entire goddam 36-hour shift with muesli bars and yoga exercises. An international comparison by the University of Oldenburg recently revealed that the countries with the longest working hours are also those with the lowest productivity. Business has been completely transformed; the Old Economy's input-output equation no longer applies. What counts today is the number of good ideas, not the hours you spend at your desk. Instead of heading for death by overwork, executives should think about what their companies can do differently and better. In Japan, they have a word for the phenomenon of "death by overwork": karoshi. Because this cause of death is no rarity in Japan. In fact, corporate liability for it was legally recognized not long ago – which is good news for the relatives. Cynical? Macabre? Absolutely!

But karoshi is only a symptom of the production methods of the late twentieth century. Case studies suggest that the reason for the self-sacrificing overwork in Japan tends to lie in production management.

Eighty-eight per cent of all companies in Japan confidently expect people to work overtime. One pharma group advertised a new power drink with the slogan "Are you prepared to fight for your company 24 hours a day?" A purely Japanese syndrome? Not at all! This mentality is widespread throughout the world.

You can forget "time management", that old stalwart of the self-help books. What good is it to anyone if efficient "time planning" gives you enough time to twiddle around with the little cogs, but you ignore the big steering-wheel? That's why it is so important always to start by asking the right questions. Not so that you can optimize your planning for the day, but so that you can think first of all about how you can make a difference every day.

The perfect show of professional commitment: work hard, sleep little – that's yesterday's success story. Smart companies understand that the decades-old business dogma that equates physical presence with productivity is simply stupid. Smart organizations do it differently: they judge performance on output instead of hours.

The perfect show of professional commitment – work hard, sleep little.

Yes, of course pressure has increased steadily over the past few years. The Germans, supposedly the world champions of leisure, are working ever longer, harder and more diligently.

What's more, according to the economic researchers, workloads are increasing. Those who still have jobs not only have to cope with constantly increasing requirements, but also with constantly changing conditions.

People are overburdened; they feel drained and no longer able to cope properly with the constant changes. They also sense that they could very easily be replaced and – despite "people are our most important asset" assurances to the contrary – that they are only a means to an end. Everyone knows that employment these days has become a kind of sufferance: if your company can somehow get along without you, it will be quick to do so. Once you've fulfilled your purpose, you'll very soon be out of a job. People used to be thrown out for bad work, but that's not the reason nowadays. Employees are not necessarily sacked because of bad work. Rather, they have to go because nobody needs them any more, because companies streamline processes, eliminate, relocate or subcontract parts. And it's no temporary phase, but the new reality.

Good is better than lots

"Carry on regardless" can hardly be the right response. The answer has to be "Change your thinking!" And radically, too. Work has to be reinvented, redefined, and new scope for people's development has to be created. And it is the responsibility of the managers to take the lead here. Managers who work smart instead of hard don't boast of their crammed diaries.

The salaryman is an obsolescent model.

A while ago, we were in Japan. A young university professor told us of his father, a typical Tokyo salaryman, who just stares into space like a zombie on Sundays when at home with his family, in a state of total physical and mental exhaustion. He goes to the office by underground every morning at six, then works in an open-plan office, constantly under the watchful eye of the boss, until nine o'clock at night. Then the whole team goes to the karaoke bar. Anyone who misses the last train home can spend his few hours' rest in a hotel with rooms the size of luggage lockers. The salaryman is an obsolescent model. If you're nailed to the floor by your work you can no longer think clearly. Human robots cannot be creative.

Above all: they have no fun. In the coming years, management also means giving people back their joy in work. Otherwise, we really will run out of work, as pessimists have been foretelling for years. Not because there's nothing to do. But because no one will be able to force himself to do it. Two business thinkers from Scandinavia, Jonas Ridderstråle and Kjell Nordstroem, call out Nietzsche's words to their readers: "Work is pleasure!" And they say "In order to be creative, we have to be relaxed. We need time to sit down, think, play around and experiment."

In order to be creative, we have to be relaxed.

In the foreseeable future it's unlikely that many managers will be doing what Red Bull inventor Dietrich Mateschitz does and working only three days a week. But they might discover that there comes a point where hard work and creativity need not necessarily be in conflict. Picasso is a very good example. There is practically no museum in the world with sufficient rooms to stage an exhibition of Picasso's complete works. He simply painted far too much for that. In this sense, Picasso, in contrast to Vermeer, for example, was a hard-working and highly productive artist.

However, Picasso also regularly switched to doing something new. And not because the old stuff was bad. The early pictures of the "Blue Period" or the "Rose Period" are fascinating masterpieces. Picasso could have taken the easy way and stuck with them. No gallery owner asked him to invent Cubism. On the contrary, gallery owners and art purchasers love it when an artist always paints more or less the same thing. Like Jan Brueghel the Elder, that scion of the famous dynasty of painters who plastered the walls of aristocratic European palaces with bouquets of flowers painted in oils. Picasso didn't specialize in harlequins to the point of market saturation, but constantly reinvented himself as an artist. That's why Picasso exhibitions today draw hundreds of thousands of visitors.

Managers who work smart, not hard, are anything but lazy. They know how to do the right things. Gone are the days when the man with the most beads of sweat on his brow or the fastest pulse was the most useful to the company. Nowadays, the central question is where new, clever ideas come from. Working smart, not hard, therefore also means being an information junkie. It is absolute nonsense to say that managers are drowning in a flood of information. We don't have too much information. As a rule we have far too little. That is why it's so important to be constantly sucking in ideas with your antenna quivering. And we have to shift our behinds, to be outside and on the ground, talking to our customers and constantly gathering information.

Oh, yes, before we forget, let's go back to the subject of sleep deprivation. In a recent *Wirtschaftswoche* article, the famous sleep researcher Juergen Zulley gave comfort to all those hard-working people who can only get to sleep with a guilty conscience. The need for sleep is an individual, innate predisposition that is almost impossible to influence deliberately. If you still want to wean yourself off sleep, think carefully before you do. Because in the long term, getting too little sleep makes you "fat, stupid and sick", in Zulley's provocative words. What's more, sleep deprivation shortens your life. Film director Rainer Werner Fassbinder, for example, had nothing but contempt for sleep and said: "I can sleep when I'm dead." He died at the age of 37. So, do something with your life. But sleep well.

PART ③

FROM JOB-HOLDING TO VALUE DELIVERY

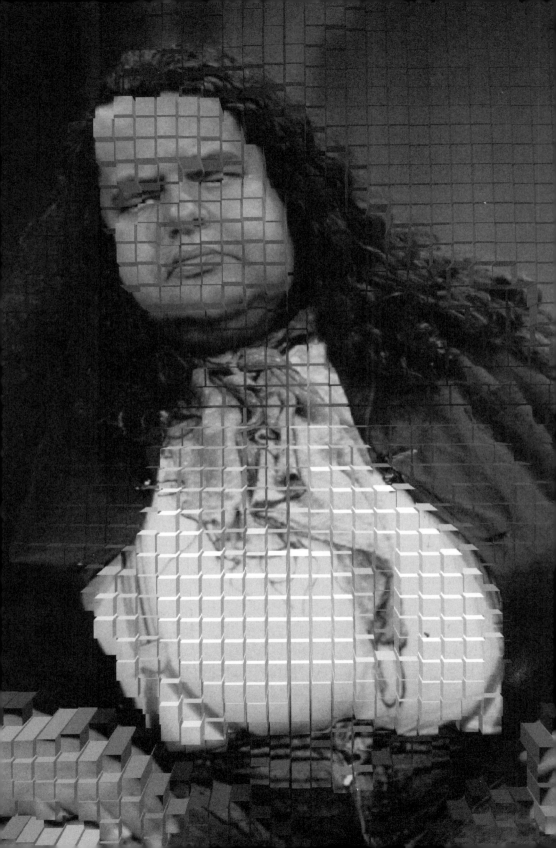

CHAPTER 18

FAILED: DOCILE, OBEDIENT, USELESS

Once upon a time, Mr Jones, Head of Department X, drove to the airport in his car, parked there – an expensive undertaking – flew to Zurich, took a taxi to the Congress Centre, then went on to a hotel, and did the same trip in reverse the next morning. Then he reclaimed his expenses, and he wanted the cash in his account by the day after tomorrow if at all possible.

The Travel Expenses Department was responsible for the reimbursement. Portly middle-aged men sorted, copied, checked, stamped, filed, entered all the receipts, and finally transferred the money. They wore knitted pullovers, arrived at work at eight o'clock in the morning in big VW estate cars, and finished at five o'clock sharp. After 15 years in the Travel Expenses Department, the terraced house in the suburbs was paid for. After that they could start saving for their retirement in Mallorca. And anyone accustomed to thinking on that kind of timescale would inevitably process individual transactions at their own pace.

Jana, travel expenses accountant with the Walldorf software giant SAP, doesn't own a terraced house and has never been to Mallorca. Deeply absorbed, the 28-year-old checks the distance from Bonn to Walldorf in the route planner, checks off the hotel bill, works through car park receipts one after the other. With nimble fingers she hammers numbers into the keyboard, presses the enter key – click, done, next transaction please. She doesn't know whether she'll still be doing this job in two or three years. The times are changing fast, and you have to grab your opportunities while you're young.

Jana's office is not in Walldorf, but in Prague. Soon, 300 employees would be doing routine administration tasks for SAP in a brand new office building there. At a fraction of Western European labour costs. That's only the beginning. Following the migration of production, companies are now relocating administration jobs eastwards by the ton. And research and development will follow administration. The first few moves are already being made. And it's no problem at all when there are 600,000 Indian engineers graduating every year. Kamal Nath, the Indian Minister of Commerce and Industry, once said: "We find the Europeans fighting for a 35-hour week, and we in India are fighting for a 35-hour day." And he smiled.

Braking in the fast lane

Did we seriously believe that people in the Czech Republic or China would be satisfied with assembly-line jobs forever? And where does it say that an Indian engineer can't have as good ideas as a German, English or Spanish one? If you have eyes to see, look around you: countries once described as emerging economies, like China or India, are overtaking us. Or, as recently happened at Deutsche Bahn, you can go on strike for a 10-year employment guarantee. The fact is that people all over the world can be just as clever, inventive, hard-working, creative and innovative as in the high-wage countries. And they're just waking up to that fact and working full out to develop their talents. Under such circumstances, getting an education behind us and then working docilely through the years until pension time is unlikely to be the ticket to the future for us Europeans. There's a strong probability that one of those 1.3 billion Chinese really will want to get on a train and take the job. There's a sarcastic comment that has long been doing the rounds in German companies: an office worker is an expensive microchip. And a middle manager is a breathing mail server. Every individual, really every one, who still wants to have a job in the future has to keep asking himself the following two questions:

1. Can someone less expensive do my job just as well?
2. Can my job be done just as well by a computer?

If your answers to questions one and two are an unequivocal "yes", you have a real problem. It's a simple question of survival whether you can do your job in a way that cannot be matched by your colleague in India and China, or your colleague the computer.

A hopeless situation? No. There is a way out. Ask yourself what you are good at. What unique and value-added contribution can you bring to the table, based on your special talents? And then make yourself into a top expert in your field, whatever it may be. The main thing is to work on it every day. That will soon be a bare essential in global hypercompetition.

But we'll discover that this really does us good. We'll be living in a world where we can finally take advantage of our full capabilities.

Can my job be done just as well by a computer?

Let's be honest: there are no jobs for life any more. That's why it won't do you any good to do your present job with docile obedience. In the hope that no one will notice you and that you will be able to wangle your way through life forever. That may have worked for some people in the past – see Travel Expenses Department above – but it just isn't enough any more. There's only one safe bet nowadays: the capital between our ears. Our knowledge and skills, talents and dreams.

These things make up our personal brand capital. We should guard it, care for it and keep developing it. But that's not enough. We have to take another step: develop perceived special features. "If there is nothing very special about your work, no matter how hard you apply yourself, you won't get noticed and that increasingly means you won't get paid much, either," Michael Goldhaber once wrote in an article for the American magazine *Wired*.

That means we all have to try and set up temporary monopolies. We have to become the expert in a quite specific field, whether it is sport, accounting, music, cooking or whatever. And after that, we have to develop quite unique features and skills, and work every day to make sure the world knows about them.

Take Jamie Oliver, the British star chef. This guy is a world-famous virtuoso of the egg whisk, a telegenic TV chef, the author of innumerable cookbooks of course – and *English*. He comes from the country where at one time the food was often thought to equate to a physical assault. To this day, foreigners who escape the minted peas or vinegar-flavoured crisps may think themselves lucky. This boyish thirtysomething was suddenly crying out to his fellow countrymen: "That's all complete crap."

Jamie Oliver is a phenomenal show talent. At the tender age of 23, he shot to fame with his TV series *The Naked Chef* and in 2002 opened the popular "Fifteen" restaurant in London. There's no doubt he's a good chef, but many, many others can make the same claim. What distinguishes him from the hordes of other good chefs? The answer is that he's not docile and obedient, otherwise he would probably be a junior sous-chef in some kitchen brigade in London. He's an unconventional thinker, and equally good at marketing his capabilities – all over the world. There's not a bookshop in Frankfurt, Sydney or Los Angeles without a special display of his cookbooks. Not a weekend without a cookery show featuring Jamie Oliver on Italian, German or British TV. Not a women's magazine that doesn't offer its readers Jamie Oliver recipes made easy.

Who am I? What do I stand for? What makes me special?

Jamie Oliver has shown everyone the way. The dreary amateur cooks who grew up with TV chefs of the here's-one-I-prepared-earlier type. The provincial roast beef fans who think Panacotta is a city in Tuscany. Jamie Oliver found unequivocal answers to simple core questions: Who am I? What do I stand for? What makes me special? The "Naked Chef" was the first of his kind: cool, unconventional, creative, casual, attractive, socially committed – and he can cook, too!

But it would be a sheer waste of time and energy to copy Jamie Oliver now. You have to find your own answers. Your personal strengths, your passion and your unique past have to be your guide. Because our lives aren't those of our bosses, consultants or coaches, and definitely not those of our personnel developer.

And once you've identified what you want to stand for, you have to keep learning, constantly expanding your knowledge in your own and related fields. Knowledge is a perishable commodity. Its best-before date will pass sooner or later – that much is certain. It won't work to change the label, as dishonest tradesmen sometimes do. Make sure your knowledge is fresh. All the time. Every day. Develop an appetite, an addiction to your fix of life-long learning. Otherwise you risk becoming superfluous and valueless. Not as a human being, but for the world of employment, the constantly renewing process of value creation.

Develop an appetite, an addiction to your fix of life-long learning

At this point, we hear some readers objecting: but what if I'm neither as attractive nor as telegenic as Jamie Oliver? What if I can't cook or do anything else really well? After all, not everyone can have the energy of a Richard Branson. Not all of us spout ideas like Steve Jobs. And not everyone looks like Heidi Klum. Sorry, but all these things are just excuses. Every human being is unique, and therefore every human being can do unique things. Does the name Hermes Phettberg mean anything to you? When we lived in Vienna, we witnessed this actor, artist, author and talk-show host live on a few occasions. At a conservative estimate, we would guess that 90 per cent of Austrians hate Hermes Phettberg like poison, yet this guy has achieved cult status.

What is Hermes Phettberg's special talent? It's to have *no* talent. The man is fat, has greasy hair and looks as fresh as a Manchester United fan after an eight-day, post-championship-winning binge. He is an actor of little talent, an artist without a deal of imagination, an author of no particular brilliance, and as a talkshow host he fumbles his way from one embarrassing situation to the next. But that's exactly what defines him: he is utterly impervious to pain, fear or shame. In a broad Viennese accent, he talks every bit as freely about his predilection for homosexual sado-masochistic sex as about every other detail of his life.

He's a living denunciation of the widespread dual morality that is found the world over – not only in Austria – and he encourages others to free themselves of their inhibitions, at least to some extent. This man is living proof that anyone can do his own thing. All you need is self-knowledge and a large helping of courage. And then you have to keep asking yourself what you will do that is unique on every day that passes.

Anyone can do his own thing.

That is, of course, in sharp contrast to the classic career path. In the old days, you could read a career path as you would a train timetable. School, university, internships, join a large company, trainee programme, personnel development plan, regular promotions, interrupted only by annual holidays. Straight ahead as if on rails, you just had to press the right buttons.

But let's be honest: all that stuff was deadly boring. So let's look forward to the future of work, because never before was every one of us able to make so much of his life. True, there are no soaring flights without the risk of a crash. But staying on the ground is no alternative. Otherwise, others will conquer space.

CHAPTER 19

INDIVIDUALITY: COMPANIES NEED GUERRILLA FIGHTERS, NOT SOLDIERS

It was 1987. Regine Stachelhaus was a petite young lawyer working in the legal department of the up-and-coming IT company Hewlett-Packard in Germany. She really wanted to throw herself into her career, but she had a problem. A male problem with a tremendously powerful pair of lungs. She had become the mother of a son, had taken parental leave – and that leave was now over.

In the mid-1980s, it was still taken for granted by most people in West Germany that men pursued careers and women brought up children. Regine Stachelhaus wasn't about to put up with that. She wanted both. So she suggested to HP that they should set up childcare facilities. Her bosses – all men – thought that was nonsense. But she didn't give up. She secretly visited the wives of the directors and got them enthusiastic about the idea. The subject of the childcare facilities was dished up at the managers' breakfast table. And the suburban villa pressure group got its way. Soon after, Regine Stachelhaus's idea became reality.

This was a double victory for her career. She knew that her son was well taken care of, and at the same time it got people talking about her in the company. All the managers at HP Germany now knew her name and had experienced a taste of her assertiveness. In the year 2000, Regine Stachelhaus became managing director of Hewlett-Packard Germany's Imaging and Printing Group (IPG), which generated around 2 billion euros a year – a good third of the company's total revenue – selling mainly printers, scanners and digital cameras. When anyone talks to this high-powered career woman about the company childcare facilities, her first major coup, she smiles and says: "I suppose that's what you would call guerrilla tactics nowadays."

The loyal opposition

Guerrilla? It has a militaristic sound, but the metaphor hits the nail on the head. If you want to be successful in tomorrow's world of employment, you can't be satisfied with the role of the little soldier who stands to attention and reacts on the "command and control" principle. Nowadays, you're better off being an independent, skilled guerrilla operator than an obedient soldier.

A guerrillero is not an anarchist.

This doesn't mean that the new-style employee constantly disregards his boss's wishes. A guerrillero is not an anarchist. Riot is not his aim. Rather, he is a passionate fighter for a legitimate objective. He is egoist and altruist in one, if you so wish. Regine Stachelhaus did something not only for her own career but also for women's opportunities at HP, and for the compatibility of a family and a career. There was absolutely no conflict in what she undertook to do between her own interests and those of other women. To reach her legitimate objective, she did not avoid conflict. But she didn't seek frontal confrontation either. She "ambushed" her opponents, or in other words, used guerrilla tactics.

The corporate guerrillero is an intelligent sparring partner for his bosses whose ideas help them to make progress. People who think for themselves are needed, because no boss knows it all or has a monopoly on the best and brightest ideas.

So guerilleros fight simultaneously for themselves and for their company. They prevent it from slumping into mediocrity, and form a kind of loyal opposition within the firm. This loyalty is primarily devoted to the success of the company, and only goes to a specific boss after that. Just as emancipated citizens don't pledge allegiance to a specific politician, but solely to the democratic state and its constitution.

And just as emancipated citizens can obtain information themselves and arrive at political judgements independently of party rhetoric, the new-style employee has his own opinions. He gathers information independently instead of just carrying out his boss's orders to the letter. He argues with him on a level of equals, instead of flattering his superior's inflated ego. He thinks for himself instead of puzzling over what the boss wants to hear.

It sounds like damned hard work. So at this point you may be wondering why you should do that to yourself. Why put up a fight if you can just swim with the tide? In that case, may we first remind you politely but firmly of the 1.3 billion Chinese (see Chapter 18) who are in the water along with you. At least one of them is burning to do your job. And would do it as well as you in two, three years at the most. You can depend on that. Or you can go on strike.

Why put up a fight if you can just swim with the tide?

But as always, compulsion pure and simple is a bad motive for change. Things rarely happen without pressure, though, so we should be glad that the Chinese, Indians and other emerging industrial nations are exerting plenty. It is, however, up to us to develop positive aims. American writer and philosopher Ralph Waldo Emerson once said: "There are always two parties, the party of the past and the party of the future; the establishment and the movement." It's your choice.

Only movement creates satisfaction. Nature never intended human beings to hibernate. So it's time to wake up. The company is you! You have to do something. Not the head of department. Not the managing board. Not the politicians. When people demand that "the others" should change, it's never anything but an excuse.

Only movement creates satisfaction.

Forget the Dilbert principle – always complaining about "the others", "the system", the company where nothing works. Surviving with an XXL helping of cynicism in a system that you can't change anyway. Awfully amusing, isn't it? Dilbert is not amusing. Dilbert is a wet, a wimp, someone who seeks refuge in inner emigration through cynicism. That sort definitely don't help to make the world a slightly better place. They would do better to follow Birka Schmittke's example.

Who decrees how a school has to operate?

Birka Schmittke is a teacher in Berlin. To be more precise, she is the head teacher of a secondary school in Berlin. Oh my God, you're thinking, she hasn't exactly landed in a bed of roses. Head of a school, in Berlin of all places. We've all heard the stories about the problem cases. But Birka Schmittke's school, the Georg-Weerth-Realschule, is completely different in many ways. It isn't just some grey educational institution made of ugly concrete, where poorly motivated youngsters go for an official stamp on the way they spend their mornings. This school is a professional service company. And that's why Birka Schmittke and her school have found a place in this business book.

Service companies have a value proposition for their customers. In the case of the Georg-Weerth-Realschule, every customer, in other words every student, is guaranteed a traineeship or the chance to go on to a senior school. Exactly. Not given the opportunity. Not enabled. Not offered. G-u-a-r-a-n-t-e-e-d.

To make that happen, the school collaborates with a large number of companies in the region, runs job application training sessions regularly and offers classes in preparing for the workplace from Year 7 onwards. The highly regarded business club "Verein Berliner Kaufleute und Industrielle", which pursues a number of social causes, has granted the establishment the honourable title of "High-performance School". The demand for places there is now greater than the supply.

And yet the school is in Friedrichshain, one of Berlin's poorest districts. The building is totally run down; there has been no investment for years. Yet here, of all places, students write business plans. And when the "bank" – in the form of a development association – gives the green light, students set up companies. For example, an art lease firm that decorates shop windows and doctors' waiting rooms with pictures.

No Minister for Education asked Birka Schmittke to make changes at her school.

We repeat with all due emphasis: no Minister for Education asked Birka Schmittke to make changes at her school. On the contrary, she would have saved herself a lot of trouble initially if she had simply worked by the book. What's more, there was virtually no point in Birka Schmittke trying to further her career. She had a head teacher's position and was in the top salary grade. Birka Schmittke just didn't want to come to terms with a failing system. This woman in her mid-forties couldn't accept the idea of sitting in her head teacher's chair, turning into a wrinkled, grey cynic. She did something. When she took out a subscription to the business magazine

Wirtschaftswoche in 1998, it became suddenly clear to her that they had to learn to think like entrepreneurs at this school!

Birka Schmittke became a guerrilla fighter. Her reward? The success of her work. Students who now have prospects they never had before. But also, recognition. From the students, from the parents, from the business world. Well, Dilbert, that's a shock to your system, eh? One individual can change the world a little bit. Or at least – in Confucius's sense – light a candle in it. A small one, at least. Sometimes a big one.

When we talk about these or similar examples, we often get the response: great. That's really fantastic. And then the word we have learned to hate rears its head: *but*. *But* that wouldn't work here. *But* my boss is an old die-hard and doesn't want change. *But* our Managing Board has blocked every initiative so far. *But* our parent company does not want us to experiment. Duh! These are just defensive mechanisms. Pretexts for not leaving the comfort zone. And for not having to take any risks. The "but" sentences amount to: if you don't do anything, you won't start any conflicts. And after all, conflicts mean having to exert yourself.

But we can say *but*, too: *but* we don't accept that. *But* if you don't exert yourself you'll waste your life. *But* if you avoid conflicts, you won't move anything. *But* anyone can move something, for himself and others. *But* in many cases it only works in small steps. By ambush. With guerrilla tactics. We'll be happy to show you a few tricks from the guerrilla fighter's manual.

Become a business guerrillero in five steps

First, it's important to develop a clear concept from the beginning: it isn't enough to have a good idea at the back of your mind, a flash of inspiration. A good concept is credible, consistent and founded on sound commercial thinking. It has to be based on findings that are hard to attack. Facts and figures are important. If the guerrillero is not armed to the gunwales with these, he'll sink without trace. You have to be able to document that you really know what you're talking about, and that you can prove the occasional bold statement. That still isn't enough for you to encircle the enemy completely. The package also has to be emotionally appealing. People never make judgements on a purely rational basis. Your idea can only reach people's hearts if it appeals to values like beauty, joy, hope, justice or freedom.

You're bound to lose a few skirmishes before you win the guerrilla war.

Second, you need allies within your company. Individual guerrilleros who challenge the status quo and produce bold new ideas can easily be overlooked or pushed to one side. But once there are several, they are much harder to get rid of. It is also good for your own psychological balance to know that you have allies and don't have to fight alone. Because setbacks are unavoidable. You're bound to lose a few skirmishes before you win the guerrilla war. Another thought: your allies may not even need to be colleagues. How about getting an innovation going with a customer or a supplier? Birka Schmittke didn't seek her allies among her teaching staff or in the Berlin government, but in business.

Third, it is always a good thing to enter prototypes in the race as soon as possible. To act fast without knowing all the answers at the start. That's the only way to seize opportunities, move forward, fine tune while running and ultimately reach the finishing line – ideally before anyone else does.

It's often outsiders who reinvent entire industries.

In the spring of 1994, Jeff Bezos, the founder of Amazon.com, read a forecast that said the Internet would grow by 2300 per cent per annum. Inspired by this utterly inexhaustible market potential, he compiled a list of things he could sell over the Internet. It included everything from fashion to music. Bezos finally decided on books. However, it should be said up front that Bezos was not a trained bookseller, nor did he come from a family of booksellers. He had a job on Wall Street that he gave up to pursue the idea of an Internet bookstore. You remember: it's often outsiders who reinvent entire industries.

Bezos wasted no time. He made his decision without writing a detailed business plan for the fledgling Amazon.com, even without knowing where the company would be based. It sounds almost like the stuff of Hollywood fairy tales: on the day of the relocation, all Bezos had was an improvised list of options for his company location. He did know, however, that all of them lay west of New York. That was a start, because he was able to instruct the driver to take that direction. The next day, Bezos made the decision to base his new company in Seattle – and phoned this information through to the driver of the removal van.

It was clear to Bezos that if the Internet was growing by 2,300 per cent every year he didn't have a day to lose. That was why function had clear priority over style and editorial content in his website design. He didn't bother with fancy graphics and animations. What Bezos wanted was to make it as easy as possible for visitors to find and buy books. You could put it this way: Bezos sent a prototype into the race and then fine-tuned it while it was running.

In other words: put your ideas on paper, then test them outside in the market with potential customers. Why is that so important? A prototype makes an idea tangible. And it has another huge advantage: it enables you to demonstrate that your amazing idea isn't just a figment of your imagination. You can even draw the attention of potential supporters and start to spread your idea beyond departmental and hierarchical boundaries. Making prototypes also means learning for yourself, quickly and close to reality. Because big wins often come in bite-sized chunks.

And, fourth, that also means picking the low-hanging fruit. Concepts can be criticized and dissected, early wins can't. Believe us: it helps. It doesn't matter how great the concept at the back of your mind may be – it helps to start with a few small morsels. That gives you credibility and takes sceptics by surprise.

There has never yet been a victorious guerrilla troop made up of cowards.

Fifth, and last, the old principle applies: have courage! Do it! There has never yet been a victorious guerrilla troop made up of cowards. We see that over and over again in our work. Employees develop good ideas. They're cheeky and clever and ruffle the feathers of the status quo. But then comes the crucial meeting with the Managing Board when the idea is to be presented. And suddenly, everything is different. For fear of wounding the top management's sensitivities, the ideas that were once so radical and fresh are presented with the utmost caution. Things that came across as bold and courageous in rehearsals without the top management now sound as non-committal and soft-soapy as if the presenter were shooting cotton-wool balls. Every argument is put in perspective, every rough edge filed smooth, everything qualified somehow or other. What's left to get excited about?

That's why a guerrilla fighter never shoots cotton-wool balls.

CHAPTER 20

MOTIVATION: WORK IS FUN, INCENTIVES ARE FRUSTRATING

There's a manufacturing company in Germany that pays its full-time employees an average wage of just under 250 euros a month. Can you imagine it? And can you also imagine that 90 per cent of this company's employees said in a survey that they enjoyed their jobs and liked working there? No? We couldn't have imagined it either. Until we read an article about the Martinshof in Bremen in the business magazine *brand eins*.

Work for genuine personalities

Well, Martinshof is Germany's biggest workshop for handicapped people, a "sheltered workshop". An institution of this sort is obliged by law to give work to any disadvantaged person who can't find a job in the normal employment market because of their handicap. At Martinshof, wheelchairs and bicycles are repaired, and there are also people there who work for the Mercedes-Benz factory in Bremen – side windows for the limos are pre-assembled in a dedicated production hall. In other workshops, high-quality wooden kindergarten furniture or bric-a-brac items are manufactured. The works management from Daimler recently came to visit, and were deeply impressed by the working atmosphere. Martinshof has its own gift shop in a first-class location in Bremen's city centre, on the historical market square.

You may now be thinking: what about the 1.3 billion Chinese who can do all that stuff for a lot less than 250 euros a month? Of course, the disappearance of hand crafts is posing problems for Martinshof. But the managers' strategy is not just to appeal to their customers' social conscience. Instead, they try to offer extraordinary services with which manufacturers can improve their products or surprise their customers. Little things with a big impact that wouldn't be worth other people's while. For example, they stick chocolate Neapolitans on business letters. They attach decorative luggage tags to travel documents. Or they enhance cans and jars with stickers, to make mass products a little special.

How is it possible for someone who attaches stickers for 250 euros a month to be highly motivated?

How is it possible for someone who attaches stickers for 250 euros a month to be highly motivated, enjoy his work and want to stay with his employer forever? With no holiday pay. No company car. No annual bonus. It's hardly because he's a "dummy", a "psycho" or a "cripple" (dear friends of political correctness, such terms are in common use internally at Martinshof). It's because in this place, the reason why people work resurfaces. It's because they want to give meaning to their lives. Because they want to be useful to others. Because they enjoy getting their teeth into something. Because they are proud when they accomplish something. Because they want to do something good and feel the pleasure of doing it.

Pleasure or work? Why not both at the same time?

Forget Maslow's "hierarchy of needs" and Frederik Herzberg's outpourings on hygiene factors. Both theories state that people soon satisfy their need for money, and from that point onwards can only be motivated by non-material rewards like job satisfaction and recognition. But if you believe that's still the reality today, you presumably also believe that Heidi and Peter the goatherd are still merrily leaping from crag to crag in the Swiss Alps.

The reality of today is different: people want both material and non-material rewards. And they don't want these two rewards one after the other, but s-i-m-u-l-t-a-n-e-o-u-s-l-y. And the meaning of the work is as important as the money – but the two are not interchangeable. Can you buy passion? Hardly. Can you substitute money for meaning? Never.

Even the "dummies" of Martinshof are keenly sensitive to whether their work is meaningful or not. Ten years ago, one of the workshops was struggling with a dip in orders. There was simply nothing to do. The works management had the bright idea of making staff in one hall assemble components, and staff in the other hall take them apart again. Of course it was done with the best of intentions. They were afraid the otherwise inevitable idle time would cause their employees psychological damage. But the workers immediately got wind of what was going on. They were not prepared to tolerate that sort of stuff.

An annual bonus is an insult to people who are passionately and wholeheartedly committed to something.

In a modern, democratic society nobody puts up with being taken for a fool in the workplace. Including people with handicaps. In fact, particularly people with handicaps, because they understand better than any office slave in the world what work is really about: if you don't enjoy your work, if you aren't enthusiastic about your job, why don't you stop doing it? That applies to everyone.

Fredmund Malik, professor of management at the University of St Gallen, once said: "If someone has a job that he enjoys or takes pleasure in, you can only congratulate him. It is a privilege in every respect, and a rarity." Excuse me? Is that supposed to mean by any chance that only professors, top managers, orchestra conductors, star architects or rock singers can enjoy their work? "Refugee aid workers, social workers, teachers and priests in slums, doctors and nurses in intensive care departments in hospitals," continues Professor Malik, " ... do not do their work for pleasure, but because it has to be done, out of a sense of duty – even though that will sound old-fashioned to many people."

Sorry, Professor, but it would help if you occasionally left your ivory tower in St Gallen and actually met and talked to these "refugee aid workers, social workers, teachers and priests". We know some people who threw in their jobs in Germany to alleviate poverty and hardship in Asia. Why? Because a fire burns in them. Because they couldn't help doing just that and nothing else with their lives. Otherwise, they would have become accountants. And yes, dammit, these people do enjoy helping others. It is their life and their passion, and every small success gives them pleasure.

Fredmund Malik's line of argument closely follows that of Henry Ford, who once said something like this (the wording may not be exact): "When we work, we should do it whole-heartedly. When we enjoy ourselves, we should also do it whole-heartedly. But it doesn't make the least bit of sense to mix the two." Now, Henry Ford has been dead for around 60 years, and today it is rather the spirit of Southwest Airlines that prevails: Southwest says that people are rarely world class at something they don't enjoy.

We feel it's incredibly arrogant when some so-called experts claim that members of certain vocational groups could or should enjoy their work and others couldn't and shouldn't. A pilot or a conductor, yes. A nurse or a taxi driver, no. We are in no doubt that David Bradford would flatly contradict that notion. The New York taxi driver and photographer immerses himself in the pulse of his city and its people. Day and night, in rain or snow, he takes pictures of New York City in and from his car. Black and white snapshots only. Six days a week. With heart and soul. His pictures are in motion just as he is in motion himself. They are the children of a pretty "wild love affair", as the taxi-driving photographer describes his relationship with New York.

And are there really people out there who maintain he's only doing it out of a sense of duty – it's a filthy job, but somebody has to do it? Let's think of it from the other point of view: do you feel like an irritating piece of filth when you get into David Bradford's or anyone else's taxi? Does the driver want to toss you out again as soon as possible just so that he can pick up more filth on the next corner? No? There you are, then.

It is absolutely idiotic and absurd. Of course there's such a thing as a sense of duty. But anyone who has to invoke it every day from morning to night is very probably in the wrong job and should think about moving on.

Living your vocation takes courage

Or take Robert Boeck. When he left his profession to enjoy a well-earned retirement after 30 years of service, Austria's daily press found it worthy of comment. Even the Mayor of Vienna, Michael Haeupl, took the trouble to visit Boeck's place of work in person to say goodbye. Some ministers from the nearby government buildings also called in. Had Mr Boeck been a Director of Works, Chief Constable or a Supreme Court Judge? No. "Herr Robert", as everyone called him, had been a waiter for 30 years. More precisely, head waiter at the Café Landtmann in Vienna's prestigious Ringstrasse.

Living life to the full is not the prerogative of artists, entrepreneurs or inventors.

"Herr Robert" had apparently never done anything special in his life. But he did what he did in such a way that he became a legend, a cult figure, a

Viennese character. "Pleased to meet you; good morning Undersecretary; please sit here; be with you in a moment; do you wish to eat? What may I bring you?" Herr Robert knew his guests and loved people. Not just on the surface. He saw his profession as a vocation to serve other people. And that vocation starts with outward appearances: while many of his counterparts elsewhere are almost indistinguishable from the guests because they appear in t-shirts, often prominently displaying a political slogan or their favourite pop group, Herr Robert, like every other Viennese waiter, operated in a black dinner jacket.

At the same time, it was his special type of Viennese banter to call unknown guests by random titles and welcome them as "Professor", "Director" or "Minister". The joke was of course on the guests. And people say waiters are servile. And now that Herr Robert is back to being Robert Boeck, does the municipal old people's home beckon? Or does retirement on the Costa Blanca attract him? Not at all! He's starting a whole new career. He is going to grow organic cereals in his home town of Parndorf in Burgenland in the east of Austria.

Robert Boeck is a "happy workaholic", as management author Reinhard Sprenger once called it. His work makes him happy because it is his life and can't be separated from his personality. Living life to the full is not the prerogative of artists, entrepreneurs or inventors. Of course you have to compromise here and there. But all the talk about the "work–life balance" is still ultimately based on the thinking of Henry Ford's industrial age or the faded power of Prussia, once famed for its discipline and organization: don't mix business with pleasure. Everyone, really everyone will be allowed to enjoy their work in the future.

The only person who might stand in your way is yourself.

Don't get us wrong. We aren't advocating that people should work tirelessly round the clock, leaving the office after a gruelling 18-hour day with a smile playing on their lips. Even people who like their work very, very much have to realize when it's time to stop and have a break. Beware of the burn-out effect! Look out for the first faint signs and ask the people around you to tell you when you start looking drained. Because zombies make poor employees, rotten managers and sad human beings. It's up to you to create breaks for yourself from time to time; a quiet long weekend with no emails or phone calls, a long walk in your lunch break, half an hour of exercise a day ... Breaks like that are indispensible, and it seems likely that those people who love their work above all else are most in need of a good strategy for allowing themselves real time out.

The only person who might stand in your way is yourself. The art of resting is part of the art of working.

But to get back to the subject of "passion for work". There is a fire burning in all of us somewhere. But many people have forgotten about their burning passion, buried deep inside them. Instead, they do what they believe is the "right thing". And the right thing is of course defined by cultural norms and expectations. Martha Beck ("America's Life Coach") writes in her book *Finding Your Own North Star* that every person has a "social self" and an "essential self". "The social self is part of us that developed in response to pressures from the people around us", including parents, siblings, spouses, colleagues or friends. "As the most socially dependent of mammals, human babies are born knowing that their very survival depends on the goodwill of the adults around them. Because of this, we are all literally designed to please others. We are rewarded emotionally when we do it, and punished by a withdrawal of affection when we don't."

Our "essential self", however, is often quite different. What we really are doesn't take account of expectations and social pressures. And it never allows itself to be entirely extinguished. That's also why it's never too late to discover your essential self. Everyone knows at least one so-called career dropout, who suddenly does something entirely different after 20 or 30 years in the same profession. We're sure not all of these people are "having a mid-life crisis" – they've merely discovered what really inspires them.

They probably always knew it in their heart of hearts, but never had the courage to do anything about it. Like the former successful business journalist who now runs a One World shop. She earns only a fraction of her previous salary, but for the first time ever she really enjoys going to work. Or the former management consultant who is setting up a children's home in Nepal. It fulfils her. It's what she always wanted to do. By the way, these are two real examples from our own group of friends.

If you don't like your job, hand in your notice – end of story!

Here, too, everything comes down to a simple little word: courage. If you don't enjoy your work, you have to have the courage to do something different. You have to move your own behind, no one else can do it for you. If you don't like your job, hand in your notice – end of story! "Yes, but …"

No! Hand in your notice! Anyone who's too cowardly or too lazy to do it can stay put for all we care. But if that's your choice, please don't moan about it. Don't annoy us with cynical Dilbert quotes. Don't constantly rant on about the economy or the politicians or globalization. Just keep your mouth shut. The rest is your own affair.

CHAPTER 21

DUMPING BALLAST: THE SPECTRUM OF FALSE EXPECTATIONS

Once upon a time, there was a wise mother who said to her son: "My boy, go out into the world. But do not be foolish and do not get into trouble. And get a steady job so that you have security and we can be proud of you. Train as a banker!"

Her son replied: "Oh, Mother, I know that! How could I be foolish and get into trouble? How could I want you to have to be afraid for me, and how could I ever dare to bring shame on you? I have applied for a job with Deutsche Bank. I will train there and become a bank clerk, and in the end I will be the director of a department. And you and Father will be proud of me."

The wise mother answered: "Oh, my precious lamb! You are doing the right thing. You will be happy to the end of your days."

How nice the world of fairy tales is! And how nice and out of date. Of course Deutsche Bank is still creating steady jobs. But they're in India. And that's just an example. As the German magazine *Der Spiegel* reported some time ago, in 2007 Deutsche Bank had more than 4,000 people working in subsidiaries in Bombay and Bangalore. In Germany, however, the financial services provider is still busily cutting its workforce. And it's not the Travel Expenses Department that's migrating to the banks of the Ganges. That went to Bratislava, Slovakia long ago. According to *Der Spiegel*, the bank wants to move one third of all staff in the securities business to low-wage countries in the medium term.

Only one thing is certain: you can't be certain of job security

The point is, you don't have to be a German with a job in a Frankfurt skyscraper to be able to juggle figures. That's why the bank doesn't want to pay German salaries any more. "A very well-educated university graduate in India costs me €10,000 including all ancillary costs," *Der Spiegel* quoted a divisional manager from Deutsche Bank in Frankfurt; "a German with the equivalent qualifications costs €100,000." In an industry where numbers count, it is obvious that a few people will soon have to go. Those affected will be powerless to change that fact. But they can change something in their *attitude* to it. Has their dream of a steady job for life crashed around their ears? Have they realized that the nice little post where nothing can ever happen to them is the slush of yesteryear? Can they finally rid themselves of the illusion that their life's happiness lies in a tenured job from which they can never be sacked?

People used to have jobs for life. Now they have a life full of jobs.

People used to have *jobs for life*. Now they have *a life full of jobs*. Life is a project, and your whole working life is a procession of projects. That doesn't quite match up to everyone's dream, however. In the mid-1990s, the majority of young Germans suddenly announced that their preferred employer was the civil service. With a threatening new world of employment on the horizon, it beckoned as a final refuge. They preferred a lifelong civil service desk to playing job roulette with equal numbers of black and red pockets. But Father State, as the Germans ironically call it, gave his pleading offspring the toe of his boot, and passed a law effecting a strict recruitment freeze.

Welcome to the real world. But is it really as dreary as a November day in Manchester? Actors' careers, for example, have always been episodic. From project to project, film to film. Yet somehow actors still have more sex appeal than civil servants. Normally, anyway. How could this possibly be? Is it maybe because good actors enjoy the challenge, and would rather accept difficult projects than excessively easy ones? Roles that stretch them to the very limit. They read the script and say: okay, I'll do it! I'll put on 20 kilos for it, or shave my head, or live in New Zealand for two years. Actors are also *personally responsible* for their market value. It can rise, and just as easily fall again. After a blockbuster, film actors can be touted as future megastars, after a total flop viewers may not want to see their faces again for a while. At least, not in the same kind of role. Then they just have to regroup, give themselves a different look and a different image. The same normally also applies when actors get older. In the mid-1980s, in *Never Say Never Again*, Sean Connery appeared for the very last time as the gun-toting womanizer James Bond, 007. After that, it was time for the final curtain. Good old Sean was aging very gracefully, but he just couldn't play that kind of role any more without seeming ridiculous. He still appears in a lot of films. He is ideally cast as the head of a perfectly ordinary family of millionaires in Beverly Hills: still looking distinguished, but somewhat patriarchal these days.

So long as it pleases the audience, because they always vote with their feet. The box office figures decide whether the film earns its money. Every actor reaps individual criticism in the process. And it will be just the same in future for every worker. He will have to make his own money and can't wriggle out because the script was desperately awful or the director an absolute moron. No one will buy it. We can no longer get by on the excuse that the boss is asleep on the job, the company has seen its best days and the ailing economy is to blame for everything. We are self-responsible – for ourselves, our careers and our lives. Whether we like it or not.

False expectation number one: there is a secure job waiting for me somewhere. The truth is that permanent jobs will more or less cease to exist in the not-too-distant future. That means we all have to learn in good time to develop our own brand and present ourselves in the market as desirable.

Today, everyone is his own navigation system.

In earlier times authorities like the state, the church and our parents pointed the way for us. Today, everyone is his own navigation system. That brings us to false expectation number two, baggage that an amazing number of us still carry: someone will come along and tell you what to do. "Train as a banker, my boy!" said the wise mother at one time. "Study law, it's a steady profession!" said the fathers. "You should become a singer, you've got talent!" said the music teacher. "I'm putting you forward as the new district manager," said the Sales Director. That's not going to work in the future. And it's really nothing to be sad about. Remember: "social self" versus "essential self". How often has the well-meant advice of authority figures turned out to be complete rubbish! Don't live other people's lives. Discover for yourself what is in you.

For some time now, Deutsche Bank has been running a so-called Employability Programme for its staff in Germany which teaches employees to sell their skills and increase their market value. So that they can get jobs in the future world of employment. Sounds sensible at first glance.

And yet, it's nothing less than grotesque! The employer takes people by the hand and prepares them for the time after they've been thrown out. Basically, it is evidence of the inadequacy of all concerned. Today there should be an Employability Programme in every individual's head. And the individual is the only one who can develop it. Standard software can't be installed in your brain.

Curriculum vitae disastrous – performance brilliant

A new generation of people, determinedly going their own way, is gradually creeping onto the management floors. A good example of that is Bettina Wuerth. Her father, Reinhold Wuerth, features in the media as the "king of bolts", so his daughter must presumably be the "princess of bolts". But Bettina Wuerth really didn't like the role. Even in school, she caused trouble and was threatened with having to repeat a year. When her parents wouldn't allow her to change schools and move into a shared flat, she just dumped school entirely. She'd had enough of the Swabian backwoods, anyway. The peace movement and protests against the atomic industry offered her not only lofty ideals but also the prospect of a lifestyle very different from that of her parents. That was in Germany in the late 1970s.

The 1980s saw Bettina Wuerth living in Munich. She went to parties where the guests definitely weren't just smoking Virginia fine cut, and did an internship at a kindergarten. But after a while the old-fashioned mindset of the kindergarten did nothing but get on her nerves. She didn't want to spend her working life there. She is said to have been a Baghwan disciple back then, too.

But at some point, Bettina Wuerth realized that she wanted some qualifications after all. Her father offered her a place to train as an industrial clerk in the family business at Wuerth. On the same terms as any other apprentice. With her CV, no other company would have taken her anyway. So Bettina Wuerth agreed, completed her training with top marks, moved to the sales department and from that time forth shot up the career ladder. The former tree-hugger set up the group's new construction division and asserted herself in the man's world of the building trade. Then she totally restructured the sales function. Sort of in passing she also found the love of her life and became the mother of four children.

To the vast surprise of the business world, in 2006 company patriarch Reinhold Wuerth appointed his then 44-year-old daughter Bettina his successor. The unconventionalist and high-powered career woman who wouldn't have been offered a traineeship by any other company is now responsible for 52,000 employees in 82 countries, who generate just under €7 billion a year in revenue. And she's up to the job. Ex-head of the Federation of German Industries (BDI) Michael Rogowski, a member of the Advisory Board of the Wuerth Foundation and not famous for his compliments, acknowledges her value: "She is a very good motivator, has a wonderful sense for strategy and is prepared to take risks."

Bettina Wuerth demonstrates that if you consistently challenge the expectations of authority figures, you can even out-perform them in the end. But on your own terms.

If you consistently challenge the expectations of authority figures, you can even out-perform them in the end.

With her CV, it's hardly surprising that Bettina Wuerth gives a lot of thought to the future of employment and education. She told the German newspaper *Welt am Sonntag*: "The big problem with our schools is that they try to form average people. Children and young people have all the individuality taken out of them. That thread runs all through their schooldays, and you can see the same thing happening in the workplace as well." And she adds: "We need unconventional thinkers, people with rough edges, who show independent initiative and take risks." But surely Bettina Wuerth must have fallen completely into line by this time? Think again. She comes into the office in jeans and totally refuses to use a computer. She can afford to do that because of her performance.

Cannons with built-in bottle-openers

Specialist knowledge and industry expertise used to be everything. Now, the key is to keep developing new skills and just forget your old knowledge. The principle "Once I know everything about my field, I'll be able to solve every problem and will be the boss one day" is false expectation number three. The danger of specialist knowledge is not just that it dates quickly, but that it blinds you. People who know everything about their field and nothing about anything else are in a blind corner and neither notice the big changes in the environment nor come up with creative solutions.

Professors and business authors Isaac Getz and Alan Robinson tell an entertaining story on that subject in their book *Vos Idées Changent Tout*

(Your Ideas Change Everything). Sadly, it's a bit militaristic and liable to upset one or two guardians of political correctness. It doesn't matter, we'll go ahead and tell it anyway:

A French armaments group got the French army to test the prototype of a new cannon in the 1990s. After tests on manœuvre, the armaments engineers found to their consternation that quite a number of the weapons had failed due to damaged hydraulic lines. A big crisis meeting was called, lab tests, material tests were carried out. All in vain. The manufacturer of the hydraulic system was consulted. To no avail. The experts thought for months and failed to solve the problem.

There was one idea they didn't come up with: get a picture of how the cannon was used in practice. That was done by a simple technician who was called out to one of the cannons on manœuvre because of an entirely different problem. Scarcely had he unpacked his tools when he saw a soldier opening a bottle of beer on the cannon's hydraulic line, and all his comrades in arms following suit shortly afterwards. So that was the explanation for the broken lines. It took one man on site, outside the boundaries of the company, one minute to see what the engineers at headquarters had spent months searching for. Expertise can make you blind. By the way, the problem was solved by attaching a bottle-opener to the cannons. So France's engineers invented the first ever weapon in the world with a built-in bottle-opener. All that's missing now is the built-in corkscrew for the wine bottles.

Answers close doors – the right questions open them.

False expectation number four: you have to learn to give the right answers. Yes, indeed: people used to have to know the right answers. Today, they have to be able to ask the right questions. Questions open doors, answers mostly close them. But learning to ask questions is tricky. Our education system is geared towards finding the right answers as quickly as possible. That's drummed into every student at school and university.

They learn methods that are supposed to help them in their subsequent careers to find the right answers as soon as possible. A rigorous analysis, an in-depth scrutiny of the key ratios, and the top manager of the future already knows what to do. Course by course, the idea is reinforced: the quality of our analysis counts for more than the scope of our imagination. We waited in vain throughout our degrees in Germany and our MBAs in the USA for a course where you could learn to ask the right questions.

Innovations rarely work to academic formulae.

So it's no wonder that innovations rarely work to academic formulae. The story of Fred Smith confirms it. He studied business some years ago at the elite American Yale University and wrote a term paper on a radically new logistics concept. Packages were taking some days to get from New York to London, and this innovative idea would enable them to be carried overnight.

Smith's paper got a C grade. Quite a lot of it was well analysed, the professor said, but the overall concept was pretty unrealistic. In case the name Fred Smith doesn't convey anything to you, he's the founder of the FedEx logistics group. The idea he described in his paper worked, and made him a billionaire. He had asked the right questions. Among them, why can't a package get from A to B overnight? Today, his company proves a hundred thousand times a day that it can.

CHAPTER 22

CHANGE OF PERSPECTIVE: WOULD MY COMPANY BE BETTER OFF WITHOUT ME?

Have we frightened you a bit with this heading? Does it sound somewhat harsh to your ears? Oh yes, it is harsh, compared with what all the smarmily nice little books on the self-help shelves that call out "sympathy and understanding" have to say. But whether we pack this question in cotton wool, wash it with fabric softener, perfume it – or try the direct approach: we want an answer, if you please! Does the value I deliver to my company exceed my cost? Do I help others to be productive, or do I keep them from their work?

It's tough. But we think it's much better for you to ask yourself this question *today* than to have your boss asking himself the same question about you *tomorrow*. And believe us: *he* won't shy away from it, and neither will your company and its investors. You're superfluous in your job unless you really deliver value to your company, your team and your customers. That is the only way you'll earn your pay cheque.

It's not only products that have life cycles. Individual careers do as well. Every product, however good, reaches the point of diminishing returns eventually. And every career, however good, will take a downward turn after a few very successful years. It's like gravity and flying: what goes up must always come down. That, too, is an unpleasant truth. And somehow the power of gravity has got stronger in the last few years.

A career is like gravity and flying: what goes up must always come down.

There was once a gifted young economist who saw a brilliant academic career ahead of him. His dissertation supervisor had the following well-meant advice for him: "If you want to achieve anything in the academic world, be careful, because there's a lot of jealousy around. Never break new ground at the start of your career! You have to earn that right over the years. Until you start going grey at the temples, you're only allowed to further develop your colleagues' established theories and you have to try to get as many articles as possible published by leading journals."

It's an ungrateful world: the young economist cast this wise advice to the winds. He wanted more out of life than to do as he was told for years, publish a few articles in obscure academic journals and walk other people's intellectual paths. He wanted to help companies to depart from their accustomed ways of thinking. Show them how to conquer tomorrow's markets. So his academic career was over before it had really begun. His mother – among others – thought his decision was completely crazy. But one thing was certain: academia was better off without him. And he was better off without academia.

That young economist is one of the authors of this book. And if he had never asked himself whether the academic world would be better off without him, instead of this book he would now be composing some boring academic treatise for a conference where grey-templed gentlemen wearing grey suits deliver papers telling each other things they've known for years. He's never regretted that decision. If you ask him about his recipe for success, he'll reply: "My success as an author and management consultant is entirely based on the fact that I junked all my dissertation supervisor's well-meant career tips and followed my own convictions. I gave myself an honest answer to the question of whether my employer would be better off without me, and acted on it."

The burden of proof is entirely on you.

This kind of mindset also means that we have to revisit the "Skills" section of our CV every day. Are you beginning to see why you get further with this kind of attitude? And not with the "get in line, do as you're told and keep your head down" approach directly or indirectly recommended by hosts of career advice books? In all honesty, if you want to provoke us just show us a career advice book. That triggers an involuntary reaction of snorting, pawing the ground and lowering our horns for the charge.

It's like this: if you work every day on becoming the most inconspicuous element in the corporate mechanism, so inconspicuous that you're no longer noticed, you are definitely not guaranteeing yourself a long shelf-life in the organization. The opposite is true: you're documenting the fact that you can be replaced without difficulty at any time. The only way to avoid this exchangeability is to prove with every day that passes that your company is better off with you than without you. The burden of proof is entirely on you.

For simplicity's sake, start with today. What value did you create today for the future of your company? The question is the same regardless of whether you're the owner, the managing director or a processing clerk. Did you shine today only by turning up, making a few phone calls and answering the emails in your in-tray? Don't try and tell us that you've been a reliable employee and done your day's work. That's not the point here. That's the minimum you have to do to sustain your chances of staying with your company. But it's by no means everything.

The point is to make your company future-proof. To think constantly about how you can change the status quo and catapult the place into a successful next decade. Do you see now why you can't achieve that process as a nameless little soldier who marches wordlessly to the big organization's tune? These days, swimming inconspicuously with the big current of the tide is a long way short of enough.

The employment market of the value destroyers

It's part of our job to deal with a wide variety of different companies and their staff day in day out, week after week. Sadly, time and again we encounter employees the company would never miss. In many cases, the organization would even be better off if these people weren't there. A diplomat might not have said that, but it's the truth. We meet these guys everywhere – from the board level to the warehouse.

These people not only fail to add value to their company, they suck value out of it. And at the expense of all the other employees who ultimately have to compensate for their negative value contribution. Oh, my God. Are we allowed to put that on paper? Is it heartless and "unfair"? No. It isn't. Whereas on the other hand, it's definitely not "fair" for one person to cheat his way comfortably through life at another's expense. At all events, someone who is really worth his wage is much "fairer" to his colleagues.

Throw all your career advice books into the recycling bin.

We are convinced that in future any employee appraisal has to be chiefly concerned with whether this person has made a positive value contribution to the company, and how much that contribution is. At present, the main thing that counts is how fast an employee integrates into the corporate structure, falls into line, goes with the flow. This attitude leads straight to exchangeability. Instead of being an irreplaceable individual, you vanish into the mass, become first mediocre and then unemployed at some point – i.e. the very second you become the one cog in the wheel that can be replaced by a cheaper one. That's why you should throw all the career advice books you possess into the recycling bin. Take your life into your own hands.

If you don't, you'll suffer the same fate as our friend Dirk. He was every personnel manager's dream: polite and well turned out, perfect manners, intelligent, always had the right answer. He was just superb. Business degree, great. Good reputation. Fantastic. Internships with L'Oréal and Roland Berger. Admirable. The big names. Perfect. Thanks to a few semesters abroad, fluent in English. Wonderful. And of course a master of anything to do with computers. Everything an employer could want. As soon as he completed his degree, Dirk started as a trainee with a big German industrial company. Nothing could go wrong after that. Then came the dream wedding to Katharina, a very pretty flight attendant. Bingo.

He had done everything right – but he still got the boot.

Dirk started his career in the purchasing department of a corporate group. The Audis he drove got fatter and fatter. So did his paunch. Dirk never got out of line and always executed his work correctly. Everything went perfectly for seven years. Until the day the company restructured and Dirk was thrown out. Dirk's world had turned upside down. He had done everything right – but he still got the boot. There were no complaints about either him or his work – but his job was still down the drain.

Dirk had stepped right into the trap. He had done everything "right", and in the end all his beautiful career planning somehow seemed "wrong". His problem was that in today's employment market you have to be able at all times to explain what your value to your company is. And unfortunately, Dirk was unable to do that at the crucial moment. It doesn't mean his work was bad. It just means that he couldn't make any contribution in his position that would have enabled his boss to say: man, if we didn't have Dirk we would really be in a mess.

It's not just ordinary white-collar workers who have to brace themselves for the question of whether their company would be better off without them, but top managers as well: when Thomas Middelhoff took over as CEO of retail giant KarstadtQuelle AG, one of his first acts in office was to make a radical clean sweep on the management levels. A lot of highly paid executives were banished into the wilderness. Presumably, Thomas Middelhoff simply hadn't been given an answer to the question: "Why is Karstadt better off with you than without you?"

It really is a damn brutal question. Swap "Karstadt" for the name of your choice, give yourself an honest answer, and you'll see why we're so insistent about this. Your bald answer goes right to the heart of the problem. For example: why is your partner better off because of you? Why are your children happier because you're there than if you weren't? Why is the world a better place because of you – at least the tiniest little bit? Yes, the truth can hurt. But pain stimulates change.

Can you pass the Accenture test?

Are you familiar with the Accenture test? The global management consultancy Accenture is a state-of-the-art service group. Each of its consultants updates his or her CV at least twice a year. On these occasions, they have to answer the following questions: what projects did you work on in the last six months? What new responsibilities did you take on in these projects? What new knowledge have you acquired? And what value have you created for the company and our clients?

What would your answers be? What projects have you got to show for the last – let's be generous – twelve months? Can you explain what you've learned, and how your new learnings have increased your value? Can you explain how your new knowledge will take your company and your clients forward? Can you prove what new value you have created for the company and its clients?

If you're now thinking, "Okay, I could try this test thing", then forget it! Don't even bother to start if all you want to do is try it. We hate the word *try*. When you tell someone you'll try to drop in on his party, do you actually make that effort? Probably not. *Try* is a word you use when you want to put action off for a bit … try is nothing but a polite excuse for not doing something. Just don't do it, and admit it openly! Good old Henry Ford got it right: "You can't build a reputation on what you are going to do." You need to act.

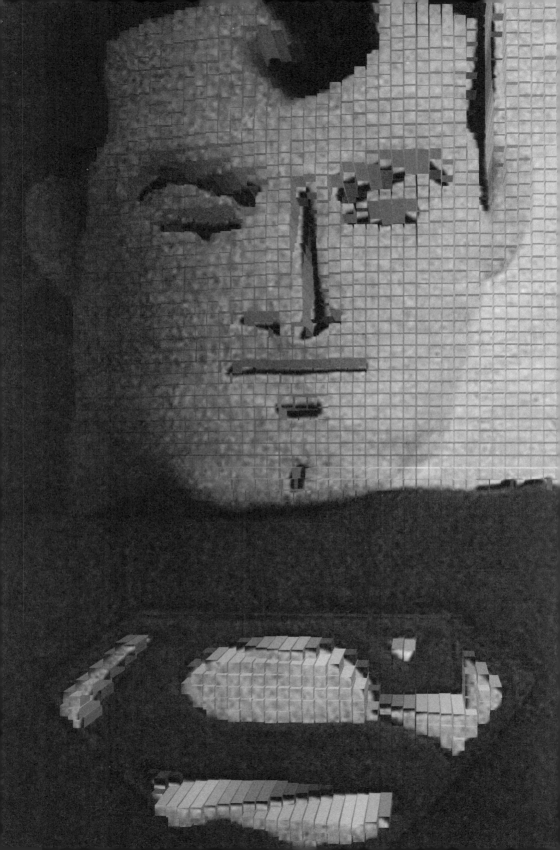

CHAPTER 23

WE CAN DO IT DIFFERENTLY: UNIQUE CAPABILITIES, NOT JOB SPECIFICATIONS

What applies to national economies applies to companies as well. And what applies to companies applies to their managers as well. And what applies to managers applies to all employees as well, to every player in the employment market. And what applies to every player applies to us and to you as well, i.e.: success grows out of u-n-i-q-u-e-n-e-s-s.

Only people who stand out from the crowd can communicate their value credibly to employers, customers and partners. Doing their work reliably isn't enough any more. And the virtues of hard work and effort are sound and important, but no longer enough. Being docile and conscientious and hard working – fantastic characteristics, but no longer sufficient. Particularly if what you do is the same thing as everyone does. Individuals who are replaceable will be replaced eventually.

For that reason, we all have to work every day anew on developing unique skills and an unmistakeable style. Unfortunately, copying other people just won't work. It can't be repeated often enough: people are individuals. Every human being is different, every human being has unique talents and capabilities. And he has to develop them actively and effectively. If you just want to stand there till others come along and tell you what to do or not do, you'll have had a fairly long wait even in the past – and you'll wait even longer in future.

Individuals who are replaceable will be replaced eventually.

What has changed? What makes the difference? Formerly, the world of employment worked by rules that mirrored those of the army. Right at the top, the Minister of War and the generals decided not only on strategy but also on the details of its execution. Right at the bottom, the battle was **185** fought. Strict hierarchies and command structures and precise allocation of roles to each individual were aimed at creating an efficient army in which thousands and thousands of people responded like clockwork. Uniforms and marching in step were indispensible components of this system. The more each person's individuality was wiped out, the better the whole thing worked.

World without borders

Many companies are still closely tied into military vocabulary today: strategy, front-line sales, discount war, staff department, conquering or retreating from markets. Fine, these are metaphors. But the so-popular "job descriptions" are still aimed at recruiting loyal soldiers for the company. Employees who know their role and execute the generals' orders.

The problem is simply that the deindividualized way in which military people think and act only ever works within a closed system where everyone sticks to the same rules. Why do the world's mightiest armies fail in third world countries? Because even the best-oiled military machine doesn't stand a chance against guerrilla fighters. Because people who pursue their own ideals and are self-motivated are always stronger than people who march in step on command. Because the freedom of the individual unleashes more power than any command structure.

Well, metaphor or no, we've no desire to wage war. The important thing here is the following principle: people are the recipe for success. And that applies particularly in business.

As globalization progresses, we are seeing our so carefully installed industrial and power systems being wiped out. The old rules suddenly no longer apply. On the contrary: progress is only possible when we break the rules intelligently. And more and more organizations, executives and individuals are realizing that. Working life is changing irreversibly all over this earth. Because people throughout the world are discovering the opportunities of their freedom, developing and applying their individual capabilities. And because, at the same time, this world is completely open and connected. Just as the famous flapping of a butterfly's wings in the Amazon is said to influence our weather in Europe, a brilliant idea by one individual in Jakarta can influence prices on Wall Street.

The opportunities of this new world are now understood all around the globe. "The people that matter in the global 21st century will be globally mobile nomads who apply their knowledge and capabilities wherever it makes most sense." These words don't come from an American business guru, but from Sheika Lubna al-Qasimi, Minister for Economy and Planning of the United Arab Emirates – a Muslim woman who grew up in a strictly authoritarian and hierarchical society.

••

The age of life-long servitude in a large corporation is drawing to a close. Thank God for that.

••

The age of life-long servitude in a large corporation is drawing to a close. Thank God for that. The average career path of the future will consist of two or three "professions" and half a dozen or more employers. You can lament this new reality – or see it as an opportunity and start to take your life into your own hands.

We all have to implement in practice what management thinkers Jonas Ridderstråle and Kjell Nordstroem have described as "Me Incorporated". We should all start to think entrepreneurially for our own selves. According to the two Scandinavians, we have to see ourselves as firms, with our own balance sheet and brand name. We have to invest in ourselves and market ourselves. Instead of looking out for a secure job, people who have understood this principle try to stay ready for action. They keep educating themselves and constantly acquire new skills in order to be the candidate of choice for potential employers at all times.

A Life Less Ordinary

Ridderstråle and Nordstroem go straight to the heart of the matter. The point is to develop unique capabilities and offer our portfolio of competences. To keep adding to our knowledge, recognizing our personal strengths and developing them further with every day that passes. There is no objective measure. Everyone starts out with nothing but a set of characteristics. Whether a certain characteristic is a strength or a weakness depends on the context. That's why every individual has to keep searching for exactly the right environment for him personally. This process has nothing whatsoever to do with the old model of a well-oiled cog fitting obediently into a given corporate wheel.

Jim Cramer used to be that sort of cog. The American, born in 1955, completed his Harvard degree with magna cum laude and then acquired a doctorate in law from the Harvard Law School. With all these academic honours he moved to New York to join Goldman Sachs. Clad in a dark grey suit, he took the subway every morning at 7 a.m. to get to his little desk in Manhattan, where he worked to fill his bosses' coffers until late into the night. In 1987 Cramer had had enough. He founded his own hedge fund. Over the next 13 years, Cramer made an average net profit of 24 per cent per annum after all taxes and deductions. At the end of 2000, when the S&P 500 was down by 11 per cent and the Dow Jones Industrial Average by six per cent on the year, Cramer made a net profit of 36 per cent. But all that is now history.

"Booyah!"

Today, Jim Cramer yells "Booyah!" in front of live cameras in his own television show. That's one of his trademarks. Another is that shortly before the climax of the broadcast he takes his chair and throws it across the studio. "Booyah!" And every time one of the people calling in to the live investment show mentions Cramer's book *Sane Investing in an Insane World*, he takes a copy of it from a pile and throws it. "Booyah!"

Appropriately enough, Cramer's show is called *Mad Money*, and US cable and satellite station CNBC has been broadcasting it since 2005. Cramer's interpretation of "mad money" is money you have left over at the end of the month when all bills are paid, all purchases made and enough reserves put by for your retirement and a rainy day. Cramer explicitly advises people not to speculate with money they might need elsewhere. But there is one thing above all else that you should do with "mad money": have fun. Every evening at 6 p.m. Eastern Time Cramer will tell you live on air how to do it. "Booyah!"

Former employees relate how Cramer used to throw telephones or computers across the office in his investment firm when he was unhappy with a deal. Today, the TV station is happy to pay for the ruined furniture, because the ratings are fantastic. *Mad Money*, however, is far from owing its unique position solely to its mad host. The show is fundamentally different from the other business programmes on CNBC, or for that matter any typical stock market news on the radio or TV or in the newspapers.

Cramer's purpose is not just to report on the current highs and lows of the stock markets that no layman can get his head round anyway. His aspiration is to enable viewers to make long-term investments and give them a feel for investment strategies. His old investment firm is sufficient proof that he himself has the knack. Now he combines his deep knowledge with entertainment. And he really loves what he does.

Added to this is skilled direction, with a Steadycam filming him with a fish-eye lens, mostly from below, and zooming in on his face when he shouts "Buy!" or "Sell!" across the studio. There are also more than 60 sound effects in the show: an explosion, a dog barking, a toilet flushing, a car crash, a guillotine, the Hallelujah Chorus, applause – depending on the performance of the stock under discussion.

You don't have to like Jim Cramer. That's not the point. But seeing what an unobtrusive financier in a mousy grey suit can make of his life might give you pause for thought. Cramer, who grew up in small-town Pennsylvania, managed to get to Harvard because he wanted to learn. With first-class legal qualifications he went to New York because he found the stock exchange more exciting than a law firm. His own company gave him the opportunity to play the wild child. But his TV show made him a cult figure. And yet, even *Mad Money* won't run forever. Then Jim Cramer will just do something new.

Thank you, Mr Jobs.

Steve Jobs, the Apple boss, once called it "connecting the dots". Jobs used these words in June 2005 in a commencement speech at Stanford University. The entrepreneur *pur sang* doesn't have a university degree himself. But on that summer day, he managed to give the graduates of this elite university something to take away that they had probably never got from any of their lectures. Maybe you read about this speech in the press, maybe not. It impressed us so much that we decided to close this book with the following extracts from it. Thank you, Mr Jobs, for these words:

… Today I want to tell you three stories from my life … The first story is about connecting the dots.

… My biological mother was a young, unwed college graduate student, and she decided to put me up for adoption … My biological mother later found out that my mother had never graduated from college and that my father had never graduated from high school. She refused to sign the final adoption papers. She only relented a few months later when my parents promised that I would someday go to college.

And 17 years later I did go to college. But I naively chose a college that was almost as expensive as Stanford, and all of my working-class parents' savings were being spent on my college tuition. After six months, I couldn't see the value in it. I had no idea what I wanted to do with my life and no idea how college was going to help me figure it out. And here I was spending all of the money my parents had saved their entire life.

So I decided to drop out and trust that it would all work out okay ... Looking back it was one of the best decisions I ever made ... I didn't have a dorm room, so I slept on the floor in friends' rooms, I returned Coke bottles for the 5¢ deposits to buy food with, and I would walk the seven miles across town every Sunday night to get one good meal a week at the Hare Krishna temple ...

Reed College at that time offered perhaps the best calligraphy instruction in the country. Throughout the campus every poster, every label on every drawer, was beautifully hand calligraphed. Because I had dropped out and didn't have to take the normal classes, I decided to take a calligraphy class to learn how to do this. I learned about serif and san serif typefaces, about varying the amount of space between different letter combinations, about what makes great typography great. It was beautiful, historical, artistically subtle ... and I found it fascinating.

None of this had even a hope of any practical application in my life. But ten years later, when we were designing the first Macintosh computer, it all came back to me. And we designed it all into the Mac. It was the first computer with beautiful typography. If I had never dropped in on that single course in college, the Mac would have never had multiple typefaces or proportionally spaced fonts. And since Windows just copied the Mac, it's likely that no personal computer would have them.

... You can't connect the dots looking forward; you can only connect them looking backwards. So you have to trust that the dots will somehow connect in your future. You have to trust in something – your gut, destiny, life, karma, whatever. This approach has never let me down, and it has made all the difference in my life.

My second story is about love and loss ... Woz and I started Apple in my parents' garage when I was 20. We worked hard, and in 10 years Apple had grown from just the two of us in a garage into a $2 billion company with over 4000 employees. We had just released our finest creation – the Macintosh – a year earlier, and I had just turned 30. And then I got fired. How can you get fired from a company you started? Well, as Apple grew we hired someone who I thought was very talented to run the company with me. But then our visions of the future began to diverge and eventually we had a falling out. When we did, our Board of Directors sided with him ...

I really didn't know what to do for a few months. I felt that I had let the previous generation of entrepreneurs down – that I had dropped the baton as it was being passed to me ... I was a very public failure, and I even thought about running away from the valley. But something slowly began to dawn on me – I still loved what I did … And so I decided to start over.

I didn't see it then, but it turned out that getting fired from Apple was the best thing that could have ever happened to me. The heaviness of being successful was replaced by the lightness of being a beginner again, less sure about everything. It freed me to enter one of the most creative periods of my life.

During the next five years, I started a company named NeXT, another company named Pixar, and fell in love with an amazing woman who would become my wife. Pixar went on to create the world's first computer-animated feature film, *Toy Story*, and is now the most successful animation studio in the world. In a remarkable turn of events, Apple bought NeXT, I returned to Apple, and the technology we developed at NeXT is at the heart of Apple's current renaissance. And Laurene and I have a wonderful family together.

… Sometimes life hits you in the head with a brick. Don't lose faith. I'm convinced that the only thing that kept me going was that I loved what I did. You've got to find what you love. And that is as true for your work as it is for your lovers. Your work is going to fill a large part of your life, and … the only way to do great work is to love what you do … So keep looking until you find it. Don't settle.

My third story is about death. When I was 17, I read a quote that went something like: "If you live each day as if it was your last, someday you'll most certainly be right." … Since then, for the past 33 years, I have looked in the mirror every morning and asked myself: "If today were the last day of my life, would I want to do what I am about to do today?" And whenever the answer has been "No" for too many days in a row, I know I need to change something.

Remembering that I'll be dead soon is the most important tool I've ever encountered to help me make the big choices in life. Because almost everything – all external expectations, all pride, all fear of embarrassment or failure – these things just fall away in the face of death, leaving only what is truly important … You are already naked. There is no reason not to follow your heart.

About a year ago I was diagnosed with cancer … The doctors told me this was almost certainly a type of cancer that is incurable, and that I should expect to live no longer than three to six months … I lived with that diagnosis all day. Later that evening I had a biopsy … I was sedated, but my wife, who was there, told me that when they viewed the cells under a microscope the doctors started crying because it turned out to be a very rare form of pancreatic cancer that is curable with surgery. I had the surgery and I'm fine now.

... Death is the destination we all share ... And that is as it should be, because Death is very likely the single best invention of Life. It is Life's change agent ... Your time is limited, so don't waste it living someone else's life. Don't be trapped by dogma – which is living with the results of other people's thinking. Don't let the noise of others' opinions drown out your own inner voice. And most important, have the courage to follow your heart and intuition ...

... When I was young, there was an amazing publication called *The Whole Earth Catalog* ... When it had run its course, they put out a final issue. It was the mid-1970s ... On the back cover of their final issue was a photograph of an early morning country road ... Beneath it were the words: "Stay Hungry. Stay Foolish." ... And I have always wished that for myself. And now ... I wish that for you.

Stay Hungry. Stay Foolish.

THANK YOU!

The image of two hermits writing away in total seclusion may fit some people – but not us. We need a team that reinforces our strengths and compensates for our weaknesses. So we would like here to introduce you to the "anything but ordinary" team that worked on this book project.

Inspiration: all the risk-takers who dared to be different, to challenge the apparently incontrovertible laws of their industries and their careers, and who allowed us into their efforts.

Support: Oliver Gorus and Achim Zoll. We received fantastic advice from both of them. If there are any parts of this book that you don't like, it might be because we refused to listen to them about those sections. We would also like to thank Moritz Jaeger, who supported us energetically with his research.

Realization: Silvie Horch and Juergen Diessl of Econ. To be honest, we were glad that the two of them were interested in our book project, because otherwise we would have had to publish it ourselves ☺. Of course, at this point we shouldn't neglect to mention Katrin Mackowiak, who edited our manuscript. Our very best thanks to all of you.

Other important people: Anna McMaster was behind the cover photo. We have fond memories of the photo session in Munich. Particular thanks also go to Petra Steurer, who manages our lives when we are writing or on tour. And Claudia Cornelsen, who in many ways laid an important foundation without which this book might never have been written.

And finally, our cat Spike should also be mentioned. We don't know what his contribution was either, but he set great store by getting a mention here.

BIBLIOGRAPHY

This book has been fed from many springs. We didn't invent the water, or, to quote Dale Carnegie: "The ideas I stand for are not mine. I borrowed them from Socrates. I swiped them from Chesterfield. I stole them from Jesus. And I put them in a book. If you don't like their rules, whose would you use?"

Carnegie was right. Even though we didn't borrow anything from Jesus, neither did our ideas arise in a vacuum. In our opinion, the best recipe for success is to drink everything in, think it through, add your own good ideas and mix the right cocktail from all those ingredients. The most important literature incorporated in this book is listed below. For further reading, we would like to particularly recommend the books by our colleagues Tom Peters and Gary Hamel and by Jonas Ridderstråle and Kjell Nordstroem. We think these authors are absolutely brilliant.

Books

Arden, Paul: *Whatever You Think, Think the Opposite*, Portfolio Trade, 2006

Beck, Martha: *Finding Your Own North Star*, Three Rivers Press, 2002

Christensen, Clayton: *The Innovator's Dilemma*, HarperCollins, 2003

Florida, Richard: *The Flight of the Creative Class*, HarperCollins, 2004

Foerster, Anja and Peter Kreuz: *Marketing Trends*, Gabler, 2003

Foerster, Anja and Peter Kreuz: *Different Thinking*, Kogan Page, 2007

Getz, Isaac and Alan G. Robinson: *Innovations-Power*, Hanser, 2003

Gibbons, Barry: *Dream Merchants and Howboys: Mavericks, Nutters and the Road to Business Success*, Capstone Publishing, 2001

Gibbons, Barry: *Chronicles from the Planet Business*, Capstone Publishing, 2000

Hamel, Gary: *Leading the Revolution*, Harvard Business School Press, 2000

Hamel, Gary, C. K. Prahalad and Harvey C. Fruehauf: *Competing for the Future*, Harvard Business School Press, 1994

Handy, Charles: *The Empty Raincoat. Making Sense of the Future*, Hutchinson Business, 1994

Harari, Oren: *Break from the Pack*, Financial Times/Prentice Hall, 2006

Henzler, Herbert A.: *Das Auge des Bauern macht die Kühe fett*, Hanser, 2005

Kawasaki, Guy: *Rules for Revolutionaries*, HarperCollins, 2000

Kelley, Tom: *The Art of Innovation*, Doubleday, 2001

Kelley, Tom: *The Ten Faces of Innovation*, Currency, 2005

Kim, W. Chan and Renée Mauborgne: *Blue Ocean Strategy*, Harvard Business School Press, 2005

Peters, Tom: *Thriving on Chaos*, HarperCollins, 1987

Peters, Tom: *Re-imagine!*, Dorling Kindersley, 2004

Pine, B. J. and James H. Gilmore: *The Experience Economy: Work is Theatre & Every Business a Stage*, Harvard Business School Press, 1999

Pink, Daniel: *A Whole New Mind*, Marshall Cavendish, 2008

Ridderstråle, Jonas and Kjell Nordstroem: *Funky Business*, Financial Times/ Prentice Hall, 2000

Ridderstråle, Jonas and Kjell Nordstroem: *Karaoke Capitalism*, Greenwood Publishing Group, 2005

Sprenger, Reinhard K.: *Mythos Motivation*, Campus, 2002

Sprenger, Reinhard K.: *Die Entscheidung liegt bei Dir!*, Campus, 2004

Sutton, Gary: *Corporate Canaries*, Nelson Business, 2005

Sutton, Robert: *Weird Ideas that Work*, Free Press, 2001

Taylor, William: *Mavericks at Work*, William Morrow, 2006

Utterback, James M.: *Mastering the Dynamics of Innovation*, Harvard Business School Press, 1997

Journals

Bergmann, Jens: "Die Unmodernen", *brand eins*, 1/2004

Bergmann, Jens: "Heller Wahnsinn", *brand eins*, 10/2005

Burgmaier, Stefanie: "In dieser Schaerfe", *Wirtschaftswoche*, No. 42, 13.10.2005

Fischer, Gabriele and Christiane Sommer: "Nicht immer mehr – immer besser!", *brand eins*, 3/2003

Friemel, Kerstin: "Loesung in Sicht", *brand eins*, 6/2006

Gehrs, Oliver: "Mit Vivian nach Rio", *brand eins*, 10/2005

Gorres, Heike: "Opfer des Fleißes", *Die Zeit*, No. 11, 4.3.2004

Grosse-Halbuer, Andreas: "Das echte Leben", *Wirtschaftswoche*, No. 17, 21.4.2005

Grosse-Halbuer, Andreas: "Mangels Masse", *Wirtschaftswoche*, No. 48, 24.11.2005

Hamel, Gary and Gary Getz: "Erfindungen in Zeiten der Sparsamkeit" in: *Wachstum. Maerkte schaffen, Partner finden, Perspektiven oeffnen*, Ed. Harvard Business manager, Redline Wirtschaft, 2005

Hardy, Quentin: "Google Thinks Small", *Forbes*, 14.11.2005

Hennersdorf, Angela: "Aggressivitaet muss vernuenftig sein", *Wirtschaftswoche*, No. 13, 28.3.2006

Henry, Andreas: "Mad Money", *Wirtschaftswoche*, No. 16, 15.4.2006

Heuer, Steffan: "Richtig verbunden", *brand eins*, 4/2006

Hirn, Wolfgang: "Das Erfolgsmodell", *manager magazin*, 2/2005

Huston, Larry and Nabil Sakkab: "Connect and Develop", *Harvard Business Review*, Mar 2006

Jensen, Lars: "Auferstehung ohne Ableben", *brand eins*, 8/2004

Koch, Jochen: "Der gefaehrliche Pfad des Erfolgs", *Harvard Business manager*, Jan 2006

Kroker, Michael: "Legendaere Riege", *Wirtschaftswoche*, No. 24, 12.6.2006

Kroker, Michael: "Taktisch geschickt", *Wirtschaftswoche*, No. 45, 28.10.2004

Leendertse, Julia: "Kein Blutvergießen", *Wirtschaftswoche*, No. 43, 20.10.2005

Lentz, Brigitta: "Zulieferer einbinden", *Capital*, 24/2005

Longinotti-Buitoni, Gian Luigi: "Traeume verkaufen", *Get-Abstract*, 2000

Lotter, Wolf: "Der blinde Fleck", *brand eins*, 9/2005

March, James: "Exploration and Exploitation in Organizational Learning", *Organization Science*, 2/1991

Morse, Gardiner: "Wie Ferrari seine Mitarbeiter motiviert", *Harvard Business manager*, May 2006

Müller, Henrik: "Bedingt tauglich", *manager magazin*, 4/2005

Niederstadt, Jenny: "Bleiben Sie Sie selbst", *Wirtschaftswoche*, No. 15, 10.4.2006

Niejahr, Elisabeth: "Gelernt ist eben nicht gelernt", *Die Zeit*, No. 5, 26.1 2006

Pauly, Christoph: "Ab nach Indien", *Der Spiegel*, No. 45, 6.11.2006

Pawlowsky, P., P. Mistele and S. Geithner.: "Hochleistung unter
    Lebensgefahr", *Harvard Business manager*, Nov 2005
Petz, Ingo: "Alles billig und gut ", *brand eins*, 2/2005
Pollack, Frank: "Das Lernwerk", *brand eins*, 5/2006
Pollack, Frank: "Die Milchmaedchenrechnung", *brand eins*, 3/2005
Schaudwet, Christian and Konrad Handschuch: "Bangalore in
    Boehmen", *Wirtschaftswoche*, No. 14, 3.4.2006
Scheytt, Stefan: "Grundig lebt! ", *brand eins*, 5/2006
Sprenger, Reinhard K.: "Happy Workaholics", *Handelsblatt*, 14.2.2005
Sprenger, Reinhard: "Innovativ ist, wer Innovationen nicht verhindert",
    McKinsey Wissen, 15, 2006
Streck, Michael and Dirk Liedtke: "Lieber klare Niederlage als
    schwammiger Sieg", *Stern*, 22.5.2006
Veiel, Andres: "Der Unbeugsame", *brand eins*, 7/2004

INDEX OF NAMES

INDEX OF COMPANIES AND INSTITUTIONS

SOURCES OF ILLUSTRATIONS

Anja Foerster and Peter Kreuz represent a new generation of European-based management thinkers and are much in demand as speakers. Are you planning a conference, looking for something special to offer your clients, or rolling up your sleeves and getting your brains in gear for a strategy meeting? Foerster and Kreuz will stimulate your mind, challenge and inspire you, and charge your motivational batteries.

For further information visit:

http://www.foerster-kreuz.com/e/

ALSO PUBLISHED BY MARSHALL CAVENDISH

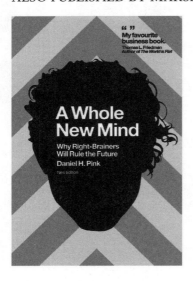

A Whole New Mind
Why Right-Brainers Will Rule the Future
Daniel H. Pink

**If it's likely that someone in China or India can do your work more
cheaply than you can, or if a computer can do your work faster than you
can, read this book.**

Lawyers. Doctors. Accountants. Engineers. That's what our parents
encouraged us to become. They were wrong. Gone is the age of "left-
brain" dominance. The future belongs to a different kind of person with
a different kind of mind: designers, inventors, teachers, storytellers –
creative and emphatic "right-brain" thinkers whose abilities mark the
fault line between who gets ahead and who doesn't. Drawing on research
from around the advanced world, Daniel Pink outlines the six
fundamentally human abilities that are essential for professional success
and personal fulfillment – and reveals how to master them. From a
laughter club in Bombay, to an inner-city high school devoted to design,
to a lesson on how to detect an insincere smile, *A Whole New Mind*
takes readers to a daring new place, and offers a provocative and urgent
new way of thinking about a future that has already arrived.

ISBN 978-1-905736-54-6/£9.99 in UK only